affinity
BEYOND BRANDING

affinity

BEYOND BRANDING

Martin Goldfarb & Howard Aster

McArthur & Company
Toronto

First published in 2010 by
McArthur & Company
322 King Street West, Suite 402
Toronto, Ontario
M5V 1J2
www.mcarthur-co.com

Copyright © 2010 by Howard Aster and Martin Goldfarb

Library and Archives Canada Cataloguing in Publication

Aster, Howard
Affinity : beyond branding / Howard Aster and Martin Goldfarb.

ISBN 978-1-55278-891-2

1. Branding (Marketing). 2. Social marketing. 3. Affiliation (Psychology).
4. Brand name products–Marketing. 5. Culture. I. Goldfarb, Martin II. Title.

HF5415.1255.A87 2010   658.8001'9   C2010-903944-0

The publisher would like to acknowledge the financial support
of the Government of Canada through the Canada Book Fund and
the Canada Council for our publishing activities. The publisher further
wishes to acknowledge the financial support of the Ontario Arts
Council and the OMDC for our publishing program.

Design and composition by Tania Craan
Printed in Canada by Transcontinental

10 9 8 7 6 5 4 3 2 1

For Joan and Jeannette,
artists who make life always interesting and fascinating

Table of Contents

part three
Extending the Perspective

Foreword

This book is about affinity...the stage beyond branding.

I started working with Howard Aster in the mid-1970s. He's extremely bright, and working with him has made me reach farther in my thinking. He's a challenge – but a positive one. It was with great mutual respect and admiration that Howard and I wrote this book together.

Affinity is about feelings, about attachments, and about bonding. It is about the "magic" that forms a conjunction, a union between people and products, or between people and politicians. It is always a combination of tangible and intangible assets that provokes affinity.

Affinity is the lasting ingredient of association. It is the epoxy, the "crazy" glue between a person and a product, or between people and a politician.

Affinity goes beyond branding. Branding is a deliberate attempt to create a relationship and to create recognition between a product and a person, or between a brand and a crowd. Over the past decades, market research has developed strategies and tactics to create brands. Every viable corporate entity, even political parties, now consciously tries to create brands and brand recognition. Branding, or the effort to create a brand, is global and everywhere.

Brands come and go and many brands try to recreate

themselves. GM today, Tide yesterday, some other brand tomorrow…all attempt to outlast the many economic cycles or demographic cycles that are part of economic and social transformations. Some brands succeed in renewing themselves, others do not.

The question and the problem this book addresses is — what lies beyond brands and branding? Can we approach, define and characterize this new territory in marketing and strategic research?

This book is based on many decades of active and varied market and strategic research with many large multinational corporations, with numerous national companies and many small start-up companies with ambition and energy. This book also draws on the author's vast political experience at the national, provincial and municipal levels of government in Canada and with numerous political parties. The effort to distill this vast practical experience and to relate it to a wide public in a coherent, approachable manner is one of the fundamental concerns of this book.

Life is about learning and understanding. Some fundamental concepts reverberate throughout this book, concepts that seem to be as applicable in the 21st century as they were in the last century.

I believe in story-telling as a creative and enduring feature of all cultures. I believe that what goes on at the communal "well" and its "gossip" reveals how many societies — especially our contemporary society — function. I believe that every society creates artifacts and totems that define collective behaviour. I believe that the collective consensus is the genius of the marketplace. This collective consensus defines success and failure both in politics and in the consumer marketplace. I believe that marketing is a force for change.

I believe that attempting to understand affinity reveals the world beyond branding!

Martin Goldfarb, Toronto, May 2010

My acquaintance and relationship with Martin Goldfarb began in 1974. I was involved with the electoral campaign of John Roberts in the Toronto riding of St. Paul's, a diverse inner-city riding with a history of swing voting. I read a strategy paper based on research conducted by Goldfarb Consultants on St. Paul's. I was interested in not just the strategic issues relating to securing an electoral victory, but also in the distinctive style of questioning and the approach to research that lay at the heart of the study. I had a genuine curiosity about the man, Martin Goldfarb, and how he understood the Canadian political world.

During the 1970s I served as a special policy advisor to the Hon. John Roberts, who was a cabinet minister in the Trudeau government. I had the opportunity to read many Goldfarb Consultants studies, among them the repatriation of the Canadian Constitution, the evolution of the *Charter of Rights and Freedoms*, various public policy questions and the performance of the Liberal government under Prime Minister Pierre Trudeau.

My relationship with Martin Goldfarb continued during the 1980s and into the 1990s. I read widely in the archives of Goldfarb Consultants and familiarized myself with both Martin's vast political and commercial archives. The archives were huge, diverse, endlessly changing. I recognized the distinctiveness of the Goldfarb approach to research, to clients, to his understanding of culture and consumers. It became clear to me that the hallmark of his unique approach ran through both the political and commercial archives.

Martin Goldfarb and I shared many common scholarly stimulants. He, a trained sociologist, and I, a trained political scientist, were rooted in a common intellectual heritage. I was fascinated by how Martin had taken these intellectual and scholarly roots and developed his unique brand of research. We decided to collaborate and write this book.

It has been an enormously valuable experience to sit with Marty Goldfarb and explore, articulate and interpret his approach to human behaviour. First and foremost, at the heart of his approach, is the notion of trust. He trusts human beings. He believes deeply in the common sense. He has enormous faith in the notion that human beings act in the marketplace out of their own self-interest. But there is a wisdom that emerges from that intersection of self-interest and common sense. He is a profound democrat. He has an unflinching faith in the democratic process and in the marketplace of ideas, of products, of behaviours, of dreams and fears. His faith in people commands him to listen, to hear them out, to ask questions, to probe, to pay close attention to their stories.

I learned a particular vocabulary from Marty. You can stretch your mind and your understanding by applying that distinctive vocabulary to many varieties of human behaviour. Human stories are at the heart of any culture. The challenge is to listen, appreciate and understand those stories. It has been a wonderful and enriching experience knowing this man, working with him and coming to appreciate his worldview.

Howard Aster, May 2010

part one

The Big Picture

chapter one

Introduction

"You have to think differently in order to do things differently."

"You cannot be an agent of change unless
you are willing to change."

This book will begin by delineating some of the varied approaches I have taken en route to understanding the marketplace. Over fifty years, I have developed an approach to market research and consumer behaviour that is both distinctive and yet quite traditional.

I have always believed that there is distinctiveness in my approach. My credo is that we are part of the intellectual property of our clients. I try to bring insight and thinking to my clients that, for the most part, is novel, intuitive and challenging. I try to push our clients, to make them stretch. That's my role, to encourage them to stretch, to go on or beyond what they think they are capable of. That's what marketing is about.

Marketing is a force for change. In that sense, it is like education. As consultants, our role is to encourage our clients to change in their own self-interest. By going through that process, I hope that our clients and their products can attract a greater share of the market and increase their profits.

My relationship to my clients has always been fundamental and, in addition, I have generally had an exclusive relationship with them. I work with them; they are my partners, as I am a partner to them. I become part and parcel of the intellectual property of the organization.

I always saw my role as the presenter of ideas to my partners. Some of those ideas may have seemed foreign, or different. But my partners learned to listen to those ideas and they implemented some of those ideas to achieve success.

Over the years, many of my clients began to relish this partnership. I provided a different voice within their organizations or corporations, a source of ideas separate from the internally generated ideas. I wanted to provide fresh thinking, an alternative perspective to refresh the organization or corporation.

The challenge to anybody who works in market research today is to push the limits of what we know, to go beyond the ways in which we think. My thinking today is pushing us "beyond" branding into an area of consideration that I call "affinity." It is this evolution of thinking that is exposed in this book.

Much of this book is reflective of the research my colleagues and I at Goldfarb Consultants conducted into the problems of our clients over several decades. I have had many clients over the years – some have been large and others have been very small. Some of them have been political. Many of them have been local, others, national, while still others have been international and global.

Throughout my working life, I have always believed that there is a profound wisdom in the decisions that consumers take – whether it is a political decision, a consumer decision or a personal decision. In terms of consumer and political decisions, I think there is a collective consensus that emerges through a process. It is the job of the researcher to understand that process, to find the trigger points in decision-making and, indeed, to influence the nature and outcome of that decision if at all possible.

One of our credos is that marketing is a force for change. By understanding the ways in which to market products, we are contributing to changing society. Change coupled to the wisdom of the collective consensus means that we move society forward towards a positive outcome.

In any research, I have always tried to present the truth. You cannot hide the truth from clients or from the public. There must be transparency and trust between the client and the researcher, and between the product and the consumer. Why? Because the collective wisdom found in the marketplace will sooner or later discern the truth and render judgment based on the collective consensus.

To appreciate how the collective consensus in the marketplace functions you must search out and appreciate the underlying values of people. Values are standards of behaviour.

Values are often fickle: sometimes they are obvious, other times they may be more complex and elusive. But the foundation of human behaviour in the marketplace is values. It is only with a thorough and deep understanding of people's values that you can appreciate the standards and the varieties of human behaviour.

What has been the single most important capacity we have as human beings? It is listening. We listen before we can speak as children. We must rekindle and preserve, always, the capacity to listen to others, to ourselves...and to the collective consensus!

Listening is the mother of intuition. Intuition is the integration of thinking and feeling.

Intuition is the path to solutions. Intuition is the source of the creative leap, the source of ideas — the ideas that make a difference! And market research is always trying to make a difference.

chapter two

In the Beginning
There Is Always the Story
...and Later...Many Stories

"Story-telling creates indelible memories...
that is why stories endure."

"Advertising is the poetry of our times."

"I look at products, be they cars, aspirins or diapers,
as artifacts of culture...and I look at marketing simply as
understanding how cultures use and appreciate those artifacts.
My job, the job of a market researcher, is simply to study and
understand people. After that, marketing is simple."

Every culture is a complex of stories, a multilayered complex of stories. In childhood, we are read stories and we
love it when they are repeated endlessly, again and again.
We become mesmerized by a good story. We never tire of
a good story.

Every society has its shamans. They are the revered story-
tellers of each society. The effective story-tellers, the shamans,

become the leaders of a culture. They are the ones who effectively reflect reality and influence human behaviour.

Everybody has a story to tell. Most people want to tell their story, and people should be encouraged to tell their stories. Today, with new social networks, this urge is increasingly satisfied. More and more people are sharing their stories through Facebook, Twitter, YouTube, blogging, etc. Story-tellers need audiences, people who are willing to listen, to become engaged in the process. It would appear that we are living in an age of the renaissance of story-telling and shamanism.

Why should one listen attentively to these stories? People reveal themselves in their story-telling. Stories are tied into the culture. Stories reveal the human values of a culture. By paying attention, by listening to these stories, you can begin to understand how the lives of people are connected to the culture and how the stories reveal the many threads, the endlessly interwoven threads and strands of a people and their culture. Every society weaves its own varied tapestries of itself through its stories. It is here that we can find the value structure of a society.

Listening to people is the key to market research. Marketing is a force for change. To affect human behaviour, you must first understand the value structure of a society. The value structure drives behaviour. It is the stories told, revealed through market research, that allow you to tap into the values of a society.

Effective advertising becomes the filtered stories told back to people in a manner that allows them to connect to each other and to the products or material artifacts of the culture. Advertising is always a function of the product's expression of itself. Advertising is story-telling in a dramatic, concise fashion and if it is effective; it has a profound effect on how we live.

In qualitative market research, every respondent has a story to tell, but that depends on whether or not there is a good listener and if the process of listening is effective. People like to talk about themselves or to tell their stories because they are happy to reveal themselves. In market research, you are always trying to find out how people make decisions: purchasing decisions, political decisions, or any kind of decision. The finding out is done through a process of listening to the stories.

Every culture reveals itself through those stories. We read Homer to appreciate the culture of his time and his society. Shakespeare, Flaubert and others reflect the times in which they lived as well. But, everybody, every individual also has a story to tell. The art of the market researcher is to listen, to discern what it is being said, to interpret the drivers that underlie those stories. Those drivers are embedded in the value system of the person because those values are the guides for human behaviour.

In listening to stories over a period of time, you begin to understand that the themes of the stories have a consistency.

To listen attentively you must be patient. The consistent patterns revealed in many stories define the values. If you can appreciate those drivers and those values, then by telling an effective story back to people, you can affect their behaviour. That is what marketing and advertising does.

In any society, it is the stories told that reveal the many varied threads that constitute the tapestry of social reality. Start with the stories told and listen, pay attention, hear what is being told. People reveal themselves in their stories and they reflect the values of their society.

The art of story-telling remains one of the fundamentals of every society. The art of story-telling in our society is compressed into advertising. Every society today is infused with advertising. The stories of any culture tend to be told today in their advertising. Advertising is the poetry of everyday life found in almost every society, much like television, the public bathwater of morality.

Games, like stories, are woven into the very fabric of society. You must study, observe and appreciate the games played in any society. And they are distinctive. They also reveal the value structure of that culture.

Baseball is the American game. It reflects the core of American culture. By studying the game, you can gain many insights into how American culture and society functions.

Baseball is a challenge on so many levels. It is a challenge between individuals – the pitcher and the hitter, the hitter and the fielder. It is a challenge of each individual's performance. Each individual has an opportunity to excel individually as a hitter or a fielder or pitcher. But all individuals are part of a team and the challenge is between team performance and individual performance. There is a fine line between individual performance and team performance and sometimes there is a demand that you sacrifice individual performance for the good of the team. There is also the fine balance between individual objectives and team objectives. Everybody tries to excel individually, but everybody is also a cog in the wheel, a part of the team. You can be called on to sacrifice yourself for the team with a sacrifice hit or bunt. There are two concepts co-exisiting together in one game – the individual and the team.

The rules of the game are the same for everybody and every team. Baseball teaches you that "three strikes and you are out." But, you have three chances to succeed. That is the American way of fairness. Try...try...try again! It teaches you how to win. It teaches you that you have nine innings or nine tries, 27 outs before the game is over. It teaches you that you can "steal" within the context of the game to gain an advantage. The idea is to be bold, to take risks and not to get caught. Playing the game too safely is not the American way. Built into the game is the encouragement to be bold, to make an effort to gain an advantage – even going as far as stealing a base!

Today, poker is fast becoming a global game played all over the world and online. It is the new American game. It is big on television. It teaches you how to "bluff," how to look "cool," how not to reveal your hand or your strategy, how to get your opponent not to be able to read you. You play your cards against your opponents and the object is to win. Winning is everything.

Both baseball and poker teach you that guilt is not part of playing fair. Playing the game and winning is all that counts.

Ask anyone in North America – have you stolen something in your life? The answer is invariably – yes! Why? Usually it is for the thrill of it, to try it and to "get away with it." There is no guilt in doing it if you get away with it. It is part of the culture and is acceptable within limits because it is part of learning the limits of the culture.

Soccer, or football, is the European game and now it is global. It provides us with an optique, an entry point into another perspective on culture. Rugby, also, can be studied and can provide us with clues into another set of cultural norms. And, of course, there is the Canadian "game," hockey!

Hockey is the most Canadian of expereinces. It epitomizes Canadian culture. It is played on ice, something most Canadians experience every year. It is a rugged game, and Canadians think of themselves as being both mentally and physically tough. Although hockey may seem rough and tumble, there is an inherent order and a discipline to it. Position-playing is fundamental to the game. There are a great many skills to be acquired, from skating to stick-handling. Hockey is won, lost and played as a team.

Canadians pride themselves on being orderly and disciplined. Canadian culture exudes a collective spirit. As a society, we work together to look after the collective whole and support institutions and policies that do so.

Winter is unpleasant for most people. But hockey is a way of turning an unpleasant climactic condition into an enjoyable experience. Canadians calmly do the same, finding the up-side, without complaint – but with lots of preparation – to whatever is thrown at them.

The games of various cultures provide us with clues as to the character and limits of acceptability in that culture. Games teach young people about the modes of acceptable behaviour. They teach us how to think in different ways. They imbue within us the "rules of the game" within which we play throughout our lives.

Another clue to understanding a culture is by studying its artifacts. They are more than objects. They embody the dreams and also the horrors of a society. We endow artifacts with our emotional drives. We objectify the artifacts of our culture and we associate those artifacts with external qualities. We make them bigger than us. We also associate our inner selves with those artifacts. We derive meaning and satisfaction from those artifacts. We attach ourselves to and we define ourselves by those artifacts. Such artifacts are the very totems of our consumer society.

Consumer society is full of totems today. We drive Mustangs or Minis, or BMWs or Tauruses. Nikes make us all athletes. Calvin Klein underwear makes us look and feel sexy. Apples make us hip and cool. BlackBerrys make us connected and important. So very many objects of our society become totems to us – objects external to us from which we derive meaning and value because we associate them with qualities we aspire to. By wearing these objects, by using these objects, by being seen publicly with these objects, we become them. We absorb their character. They are us and we are them. The totemic association is complete and publicly recognized.

All societies have artifacts, or totems. Cars are part of the totemic structure of contemporary culture. So are diamonds. They are global artifacts found in every culture. Today, there are iPods and now iPads and BlackBerrys, and BMWs. These artifacts have come to define who we are. One should never underestimate the power of artifacts in our own or in any other culture.

Culture is not just made up of ideas. Cultures are layered with artifacts. They are the "things" that give us clues as to who we are, how we feel about ourselves and others, how we derive our identities, and what our values are.

All cultures ascribe values to their artifacts. Cars, beads, totem poles, iPods…the consumer marketplace is full of these artifacts and totems. The artifacts of the marketplace are constantly changing, being invented or re-invented, changed and abandoned. The challenging question is – why and how?

Today, social networks spread cultures. People share

their experiences, define their realities and create communities through social networking. You cannot escape the commercialization of our reality because consumerism is the human experience shared by almost all. And, as long as there is consumerism, there will be advertising, attempts to influence the activity and the proclivity to consume.

The commercialization of totems and artifacts is not always a negative thing. Advertising impacts our daily lives. It provides us with an immediate and visual "take" on what we think of ourselves, our values, our sense of self and others. Advertising defines our reality and through advertising people see what there is.

Marketing begins with attempting to understand how cultures use and appreciate their artifacts. Artifacts create mantras that define an age. Smoking created a value system that came under attack in the 1980s. Its meaning changed dramatically. Big, large, fat became the pariah of the 1990s. Carbon waste is the pariah of the first decade of the 21st century. Our realities change…and as our obsessions change, our mantras change as well.

The lessons of Margaret Mead, a groundbreaking anthropologist, remain valid today. She drew our attention to the idea that varying cultural patterns express an underlying human unity. She directed us to appreciate the interconnections of all aspects of human life. Segmenting aspects of life deflected our understanding from who we are, what we do and how we function in a culture. She taught us to think laterally – to think that food is related to ritual and belief, not just nourishment, and that behind every human action lies a complex of values, culture, meanings.

From Mead and others, we learned that we can study cultural variations among all people. And, to our surprise, we may learn that cultures create holistic entities. To study a culture, you must engage in fieldwork, which involves participant observation, in-depth interviews and also some large-scale data collection. Most significantly, from Mead and others we learned that you go to the field site in order to engage your understanding in a culture. You cannot understand very much from afar. Get close to it, get into the site, and then you can start to understand.

The larger lesson is that anybody and everybody can think of themselves as cultural anthropologists. It forces one to go "beyond" the narrow boundaries of your being and understanding.

Good market research takes the perspectives and perceptions of cultural anthropology and applies them to market and consumer research.

Culture is what distinguishes us from other species. Language, symbols, tools – we use all of these devices to transmit both information and experience. All culture involves both information and experience. All of us are cultural creatures, members of specific cultures, and we are always part of specific cultures. We use, we develop in, we contribute to, we participate in culture.

What distinguishes one culture from another? Each culture is made up of specific or selective ways of acting, thinking, feeling, communicating, that allow people to distinguish themselves from others. We use words, values, ideas, meanings, experiences – language – and arrange them in distinctive and differing manners in order to define and refine our culture.

All cultures undergo processes of stability and change, development and construction, decay and destruction. The ways in which cultures are constructed and destroyed are quite mysterious to us. Yet, we must always attempt to understand those processes.

A cultural anthropologist is interested in meanings and experience, not simply information and data. He or she is interested in interpretation and intuition – deciphering the meanings of behaviours and actions.

Taking the perspectives and precepts of the cultural anthropologist into the domain of the market researcher is part and parcel of a good practitioner. A good cultural anthropologist does not begin with a model or a set of abstract propositions or hypotheses in order to "test" the model or the hypothesis. A good cultural anthropologist is more likely to shape his or her concepts, ideas from the ground up rather than from abstractions downward. Finding the right site, getting close to that site, observing, listening, trying to understand the meanings of the actors and actions...that is what we try to do.

How? Listening is the mother of intuition. Listening how? By paying attention and listening to the stories people speak; by studying the artifacts of the culture; by attempting to decipher the complex codes, words, messages, meanings, the language and languages used by people in ordinary life. People do speak about, reflect on, consider and express their own experiences.

Listening...listening...listening again...that is the key!

Life is about perception and solution. What do YOU think, what do YOU see, how do YOU see this or that, how do YOU perceive your conditions, what language(s) do YOU use, what are YOUR words?

Therefore, all good listeners start with circumstances and perception. From within these circumstances and perceptions, from within those words and language(s), they begin to identify and appreciate the problems.

Data and hypotheses are external to experience. They are the composites, the amalgams of many experiences. However, all good cultural anthropology and all good market research is derivative from perception and understanding – the art of trying to comprehend the nature of experience from the inside, rather than the outside.

All good research is about the meaning of experience, the desire to live better, to overcome circumstance, to apprehend meaning and solve problems.

That is why so much of the cultural anthropologist's craft is tied to theatre and drama. How do people "act out" their circumstances, their lives, their problems? How do people overcome their anxieties, fears? How do they catch hold of and attempt to pursue their dreams?

You learn about the culture through the stories told. And, if you are interested in affecting or influencing that culture and people's lives, the theatrics, the drama, the acting out is a way to connect.

Cultural anthropology teaches us to pay attention to what people watch, what draws their attention, what "grabs" them in an intrinsic manner. You cannot influence anything, or affect human behaviour without knowing this.

All cultural anthropology is both art and, much later, it is a science. We must "first grasp" specific experience, we must listen to each person and his or her story, and only then can we generalize. We must find their "sites" in which they act, feel, think, tell their stories. But also, life is about "living better" and, hence, the ethical imperative in all cultural anthropology is finding a way to live better.

Psychologists deal with individuals, and insight into many individuals can give you the thumbprints of a society. Cultural anthropologists, however, are obliged to look for the collective consensus that is lodged in a culture. The collective consensus captures the imagination of all and defines the main attributes of a society. Here lies the magic of a crowd and why people join the crowd.

All cultures exhibit struggles between the old and the new, tradition and innovation, the young and the old, the endless battle between the present, the past and the future.

So, you go and speak with the older generation, those

who are possessed of tradition, or loyalty or stability. You speak with them; you listen and try to understand their language. Then you speak with the other side of the equation, the young, people who are willing to abandon the past or want change. You try to comprehend their language, their words. You try to decipher their meanings. All societies are a balance – or there may be an imbalance – between these two tendencies.

Today, probably more than at any time in the past, the trendsetters, the definers of the marketplace, are the youth. The spirit of most contemporary societies and, certainly, the spirit of the global consumer culture, derive their vitality from the concept of youth. The engine of change compelling the global consumer culture is youth culture.

Youth is not just an aspect of age or being young. Rather, in cultural terms, it is an expression of joy, a desire to live and to participate in all aspects of life around you. The apparent pervasiveness of the notion of "party" is the notion of engagement with others, the assertion of the imperative to participate. Participation is learned behaviour; you learn how to participate as a child. Thus, any form of participation is an invocation of a youth culture. That is why so many older people now seek out participation opportunities. It is also tied to the notion of volunteerism. You do something because you want to, not because you must. The multifaceted presence of the youth culture in sports, fashion, health, education, entertainment, in almost everything, defines the contemporary value system.

Not surprisingly, it was Mead who pointed cultural anthropology in this direction. Today, it is crucial to appreciate the segmentation of society and, in particular, to appreciate the youth segment of society. One must look at the social structure in which young people live, act, dream, and then examine carefully the value structure within this social structure. It is, indeed, a truism that the better you understand the youth, the better you can anticipate consumer behaviour.

chapter three

The Creative Leap
Come Take a Leap with Me!

- - - - - - - - - - - - -

"Intuition is the mother of genius.
Innovation is the result of intuition."

In market research today, everybody has the same tools. Everybody knows how to generate data. Some data are more sophisticated; some are more reliable; some are more elaborate than others. But the basic tools of this research are readily known. You can learn the techniques and the methodologies of market research and, thus, access the fundamentals of consumer behaviour.

Good data, of course, give you the nuances of the marketplace. They may even give you the basis for tactical adjustments as to how to position a product in the marketplace. Data can be used for clarification, intensification, and repositioning of a product in a marketplace. Advertising campaigns tend to be driven by appreciations of the nuances in the marketplace.

Data obviously are always time-sensitive. Numbers change very quickly. Numbers give you the "Polaroid" of the marketplace…what is seen at the moment, but that fades very quickly. Hence, there is always an apparent need to generate new data, new numbers.

We can find out many things using data, but the real question is how to differentiate a product in a marketplace that is so cluttered with so many products? How do you arrive at the point of differentiation?

There is considerable belief that technology can be the point of differentiation. New technology, an invention, may give that "edge" in the marketplace. Indeed, that does happen. The problem is that as soon as a new technology appears, it can be imitated quickly. The edge or "point" of differentiation given to a product in the marketplace by a new technology does not last long, or long enough.

Intuition is the mother of invention. And intuition allows you to go beyond quantitative research. Intuition is at the core of qualitative research.

It may appear surprising, but everybody has intuition – that sense of what is "outside" the ordinary. Of course, you start with what is ordinary. You speak with people, you try to understand what they say, and you enter into their world.

The going beyond is what qualitative research allows. The researcher must trust his or her own judgment. Then, you must develop your own language to add character and to flesh out that which you sense as outside the given. Then you must allow others to enter into that language so they and others appreciate that which is beyond.

It is this intuition that allows you and your client to take a creative leap. And this creative leap puts you outside the ordinary. It gives you and your client the edge in the marketplace. You are able to redefine the marketplace because you have taken the creative leap. The objective is to convince the client to trust in the big ideas and this will allow you and your client to take that creative leap to affect behaviour in the marketplace. To do this type of market research demands complete trust between the client and the consultant.

Take one example: How do you move with your client who is making "foundation garments," a term used in the old sense — restrictive, hidden, designed to compress and suppress the body — to the stage where they dominate the market because they proclaim "We care about the shape you're in"?

Women and men cared too! In a new Wonderbra you could not just be a woman but also free — and everybody wanted to be free. The new bra, no longer a foundation garment, became a showcase. It declared publicly — look at me! It screamed out — I am free!

Our research allowed us to understand a concept — the high value both women and men placed on freedom. Once we understood the concept, we could then convince the client to appreciate the value of freedom in undergarments. The client then redesigned the product itself. The new undergarment, the minimalist "Wonderbra" was then packaged brilliantly, advertised effectively and the result was that the marketplace was transformed. The concept drove the product. The client accepted the creative leap to move beyond or outside the categories, beyond the given to the "other."

All of this happened because the client had a problem. It was trying to survive by being ordinary in a highly competitive market. The consultant said — let me go to strip bars in San Francisco and find out what men and women were seeing in these clubs. Why were they there? How did they understand the place, the behaviours, and the goings on? What were their aspirations, or dreams, that led them to look at the strippers? That was the beginning.

The result of the research was to tell the client a different story about undergarments...not the way it was, but the way women wanted it to be. The client was willing to begin to think differently. Not more suppression and repression, but the ability to undo, to release, to free the body from the constraints of the garment! The result was to take the creative leap...and this allowed the client and his product to influence the marketplace. They had the competitive advantage for many years after that product development and accompanying campaign.

In the marketplace, success is the result of taking a concept — freedom in a bra — and consumerizing it. In looking for a novel way to understand undergarments or foundation garments, you create an appetite for change.

Marketing studies, the good ones, are like anthropological story-telling. You go out to the site...you look around…you observe…you listen. You must be attentive to what is being said. You become attentive to the players, the actors, the listeners and the watchers at the site. You try to find out the problems, you attempt to appreciate the puzzle, you try to take in the big and the smallest pictures and scenes.

You must let the story unfold!

The story of the strip club visit is just a visit to one small site in a complex society. And, yet…by understanding that one small site in a sensitive anthropological manner, without numbers and data, by allowing the story to be told, a powerful insight was achieved. The story at that site allowed the reconfiguration of a company and the transformation of a consumer product and resulted in a dramatic change in the image of women that endured for decades.

Take another example. Ford had a problem and we were asked to investigate. We went to a "site" – Van Nuys Boulevard in Los Angeles. Young men were driving their pickup trucks up and down this boulevard each Thursday night. But what was surprising was that these young people had transformed their pickup trucks. They had customized them, made them different. Effectively, they had transformed a traditional vehicle into something else. We listened, we talked with these people and we tried to understand what they were doing. We probed the values which were their guiding standards for their behaviour.

The wisdom we were seeking was found on the street

and contained in the stories these young people told us. We listened, we tried to appreciate, we distilled it into some insights and we communicated those insights to our client. These people and their stories were conduits of insight — not creators of new product.

The result was that Ford took these insights that we found on Van Nuys Boulevard and reconfigured the work truck into a personal use vehicle. The researchers were not the creators of this new vehicle or product, but the insights found on the street allowed for a reconceptualization of an old vehicle into a new one. Ford went further. It then developed the personal use vehicle into the SUV. This process took some time. But Ford succeeded in creating a new product category and in dominating the market by starting with the Ford Ranger truck, transforming it into the personal use vehicle and then developing the SUV. Their success with SUVs, of course, has since been followed by all other vehicle manufacturers.

The difficulty with doing such site-specific research is that it may not be conclusive. You may well gain insight, but this kind of research does not give you hard numbers. And, usually, hard numbers give you confidence.

Moving clients from insight to having the confidence to take a creative leap is not at all easy. Many clients want the hard numbers. One can, of course, adopt a two-track strategy, that is, seeking insight and seeking the hard numbers at the same time.

How do you get clients and how do you keep them? Consultants are everywhere...today. To find clients and keep them, you must get them to buy a language, your language. If a client finds a home, a sense of familiarity with the language of the consultant, they will become "engaged" one to another and then you can share a common language.

Language is a precursor to thinking. You must find the new words, the right words, to engender new ideas. All languages are entry points into thought processes and ideas. Good research compels one into new words and new language and the task is to get your client engaged to your language.

Intuition is tied to the recognition that in life play and games are important. Think back to the stories found on Van Nuys Boulevard or at the strip club. Finding the right sites where we are able to study play and games can lead to significant intuitive leaps.

At one time, researchers could provide clients with the spark of ingenuity, with the spark of intuition. Now, most often, the creative engine of the marketplace is provided by advertising people. Researchers provide the nuanced numbers, the data. The advertising people transform this, supposedly, into the imagery that convinces people in the marketplace.

This separation of intuition from imagination is not helpful. There is a symbiotic relationship with intuition, recognition, creation and imagination.

The point of good research is not to manage information but to open up the possibility of that creative leap. Data most often don't speak. Data are not a language; they may give you a breakthrough. Data are the ephemera of a time and a place. Only intuitive judgment allows for new thinking. Of course, there are individuals who can take the creative leap with data.

Advertising is the final designation of this process to try to affect behaviour in the marketplace. Television, of course, up to now, has been the dominant mode of advertising. Television until now was the "daily bath" of morality. But, today, the daily bath is increasingly the Internet. Because of the pervasiveness of the Internet, people are their own channel switchers and their own programmers and producers of content. Morality itself is increasingly private, individualized, and self-referential. The rapid emergence and proliferation of instruments of social networking have created new possibilities for the diffusion of morality, gossip and story-telling.

Always seek out what real people are talking about. Always listen to people. Always seek out the sites where human conversation takes place. Always seek out the value matrices that define human behaviour. This starts the process of insight. But to affect the marketplace with a product, you must also have access to the decision-makers in the corporation or organization. If you become part of the intellectual property of that organization, then you can affect their thinking, allowing them to approach the marketplace in innovative ways.

chapter four

Values
The Building Blocks of the Collective Consensus

"An intellectually cogent reason is not enough.
You must influence values in order to change behaviour."

Values are the guiding standards and principles of behaviour. Every group, every society, every community, has values. And these values are reflected in everything. The values define the many ways people choose to participate in various forms of behaviour.

However, societies today, in the 21st century, are immensely fragmented entities. Groups, subgroups, subcultures, Facebook communities, blogs, Twitter…there are endless associations and disassociations and reassociations going on. In a virtually driven universe where recreation, procreation and disintegration are so instantaneous, the fragmentation is endless and the regeneration is also endless.

Two factors that drive so much of this process are the power of communications and the instantaneous sharing of images.

Images drive symbols. And symbols define values. Values

define segments in society. Today, you "are" not you by what is ascribed to you or how you are described – the view from the outside; rather, who you really "are" is based on what you are on the inside. Your value system – your psychographics – defines you and your reality.

Are there parameters to value systems? Material reality was thought to define the parameters of reality. Or, one may argue, as Adam Smith or Auguste Comte did, that "demography is destiny." But reality today, through communications and the redefinition of communications by the intervention of media, multimedia, and interactive media is much more "flexible" and "virtual." In a virtual world, the springboard for values has become extremely subjectified. Values remain the guiding standards for behaviours, but behaviours are dramatically expanded and recognized as parts of a process of fragmentation.

There is no doubt that our social system is constantly changing. Unless you think that everything, including our social system, is chaotic, that is, without any semblance of order, then you must seek out whatever dimensions of stability that you can discern. Values, shared standards or guides for behaviour, are the most logical constructs to look for.

How to communicate? The answer is that if values are the most stable elements in social structures, then you must find out what and where they are and tap into them. Advertisers are constantly seeking to do so. Therefore, they are always looking to segments in society, fragments. They define people by their psychographics and they use sophisticated radar to pick up all new social fragments that provide different or new value systems to define behaviour. Once these fragments are on the radar screen, you can then use psychographics to influence behaviour.

Value systems define and legitimize the activities of the social system and its fragments. Values specify the conditions under which the members of a social system or its fragments express satisfaction or dissatisfaction and also prepare them to make changes. These value systems limit the direction and degree of change.

Every subgroup or fragment in society today defines its own mores. There are some mores that are common to all and others that are only common to specific subgroups. We all regulate our behaviours on the basis of the values and the mores to which we attach ourselves.

There may well be an endless process of segmentation in our society today because of the advent of "virtual" reality. You no longer have to have but "one" public persona. You can "invent" endless such personas and present a different view of yourself to each public. You can attach yourself to many, many publics; you can present yourself in many, many ways in the virtual world. You can have many personalities and many faces, and you do so at your own behest. You can now create and recreate your own "self" and present yourself to a virtual public without any validation by anybody or any institution. There is today, within the virtual world, a radical individualization of the self.

However, it is still valid to argue that you should always look for the set of values that can be used as reference points to communicate with an individual or with a particular segment of society. These values guide the standard of behaviour of that segment and, if you want to affect its behaviour, you must communicate through that value system.

The real challenge today is to search for the collective consensus. One may legitimately ask, How is this possible to believe that there is a collective consensus in societies that are so "virtually" fragmented? In thinking about this problem, we must always look for that thread of connectedness that brings fragments together. It is, of course, possible to find it, but it is difficult.

One can ask, Why is it that politicians always come back to notions of "the family" or to ideas of "one country," "security," or "change"? The answer is that they seek a thread of connectedness between the fragments. Those threads, effectively, are the values that permit communication to much of society. Successful politicians seek out and latch onto the values that mean a lot to a great many of people. They find the connectors, the values that reverberate and affect people. Tapping into those relevant values allows a politician to build a collective consensus and win elections.

In marketing, as in politics, you must always find the thread of connectedness, those basic values that define the collective consensus. That is what defines success in the marketplace.

Fragmentation is only one aspect of the challenge in

today's marketplace. The other, obviously, is globalization. The pressures emerging from globalization today are enormous. The global marketplace was an ingenious creation of the late 20th century. It swept through almost everything. What remained, or seemed to remain, of local markets, to the extent that they existed, was purely tactical, momentary and specific.

Product categories today are all global. Although there is a reaction to this process, or attempts to stem the tide of the redefinition of all products by a return to localism, we live in an age where world products dominate...be it pasta, bagels, cell phones, whatever.

Global products have achieved enormous force and success by attaching themselves to a dominant spirit, namely, the vitality of youth culture and its values. It has permeated everything we do, at whatever age. Health, well-being, the pursuit of happiness, fun, success...everything has become attached to youth.

In order to anticipate the emerging value system in a society and to understand the emergence of global products, one must keep one's focus on, and listen to, the young. To anticipate the values that will become dominant in a society, one must understand the interplay between the youth and the elders of society, between children and parents, the endless struggle between generations.

Values in the global marketplace today define many aspects of purchasing behaviour. The culture of youthfulness is one such value. Quality is another value that is global. Quality can be learned. It is a discipline that is built into many global products, from SONY to Toyota. Quality is driven by consistency. All products that seek to become global must project the value of quality. Indeed, the genius of so many French, Italian, German and other high-end products is that regardless of price, they project the image of quality. And because of this assurance of quality, they command high prices. People are happy to pay the premium for the assurance of quality.

Frugality is another extremely global value today. In the age of environmentalism, and with an awareness of spiralling oil costs, everybody has assumed the behavioural mantle of frugality. Being profligate is out, wrong, effectively immoral. Even luxury now embraces the value of frugality in certain ways. Cars that are gas guzzlers with excessive carbon emissions are viewed skeptically, practically as immoral. In the automobile industry, which is an interesting barometer of emerging global values, quality and frugality deeply affect purchasing behaviour. Even expensive cars must get good gas mileage. They too must deliver frugality and quality.

Values in society are slow to change. People seek out and are attracted by consistency. They want to know what they are getting and they want to get what they know. They appreciate the bond of trust. They do not want to be disappointed or betrayed. It is this consistency that induces people to trust brands. While people say that they may like change, or can be attracted to change, they do not like to change their values. Fundamental values are long-lasting. They provide the security for us to make decisions in the marketplace, in the political arena and in personal relations. Brands promise us consistency and trust. That is why brands are so important to us.

Values are the guts, the insides, the very essence, the inner core of brands. The core promise of a brand can become the DNA of beyond branding...affinity.

chapter five

From Values to Brands

"Reality can never be fooled.
Perception is reality in the marketplace."

"You need to communicate the promise,
not just to make the sale. You need more values
in the promise to make the brand successful."

"Success is the result of preparation mixed
into the recognition of an opportunity."

Branding today is everywhere and some argue that it is everything. It may even be a cliché!

In the 1970s and the 1980s, the marketplace was obsessed with consumer disloyalty. People abandoned known product lines and sought out generic brands because of cost, quality and competitiveness. This openness created opportunities for many new products and product lines. Significantly, it also created an enormous opportunity for imported Asian cars!

It also affected political parties and electoral outcomes because there were many more "independent voters" who were open to shifting party allegiances. Old habits, old loyalties, old consumer behaviours were eroded.

These major transformation created major opportunities for some but also major traumas for others.

The result was the acceptance in consumer consciousness of the dual possibilities of change and disloyalty…but without any guilt! Often, disloyalty is accompanied by a deep sense of guilt. This is often true in human behaviour. The anticipation of guilt does moderate a lot of human behaviour and acts as a barrier to change.

But why no guilt? Because change meant striving for excellence, for better, for more. The consumer or the voter became more savvy, more tough-minded. A generation of consumers was created that absorbed both in their behaviour patterns and in their value structures the notion of change with a minimum of guilt and traumatic effect.

By the 1970s we witnessed the birth of brand. How was this a commentary on the evolution of the consumer culture and of values? How had consumer culture changed? Had it changed? The answer is both yes and no.

Yes, because the consumer culture became a global culture. Consequently, the production of consumer products now became tied into a global consumer culture. Products were manufactured no longer for a specific market but, to succeed, they had to find their place in the global marketplace. From conception to completion, in order to succeed and to have some durability, products had to be recognized in the global marketplace. Place of origin did not assure whether or not a product would sell in the global marketplace.

The world revolution in communications created a ubiquity of object recognition. Products could now achieve recognition in a global consumer culture. If a successful product could be seen and could even sell well in Peoria, Illinois, maybe it also could be seen and sell well in Beijing, Rome, Tashkent…

No, because in a fiercely and increasingly competitive global market, the success of products depended on delivering quality at a low and competitive price. This simple fact defining success mirrored the development of the 19th-century Industrial Revolution, when products and product categories had to be delivered beyond local markets at low prices and with a consistency of quality.

In the latter part of the 20th century, new technologies, information technologies and the drive for innovation gripped the global marketplace. Innovation meant doing something, everything, better than previously. To succeed in the new environment you had to find ways to do everything better than before and to deliver quality and durability at a low price. These conditions for success had to be transferable between products and between cultures. There were no longer any real secrets. What was known in Germany or the United States became known in China or Mexico. Knowledge and technology were everywhere.

Products and product lines change. But what remains

almost constant in the marketplace is the motivation of the consumer. The savvy consumer wants, or soon learns to want, and also learns to demand:

- **more for less;**
- **better than before and better than ever;**
- **durability and reliability rather than obsolescence and disposability;**
- **predictability; and**
- **design and looks or aesthetics (they are almost as important as content).**

These elements defined the new consumer and the new marketplace. It also redefined the producers in the 1990s.

The conditions for global brands were created.

The consumer learned that SONY was good, regardless of what it produced, because it delivered to the marketplace, consistently, what the consumer expected. In so doing SONY created a genuine expectation among global consumers about all SONY products. The global stamp or marquis brand of SONY was created.

In the 1990s the world learned that Germany and Japan delivered high-quality products globally. From China, the world of consumers expected lower quality sacrificed to lower costs. In the United States, the consumer very soon recognized the deterioration of quality. The North American consumer soon absorbed the lesson that US cars could not compete on quality or price with the imports.

By the end of the decade, as products and technology

became globalized and as countries ceased to be the basis of consumer choice because place of manufacture and origin became detached from the attributes of quality, brands became the basis of consumer judgments. Brands replaced the "made in" mark of recognition.

In a world where there was and remains so much change and transformation and deterioration, the intangible character of expectations that we attached to products began to define the marketplace and its products. At the same time, as the pace of change increased, our motivational need for predictability also increased. The consumer in the marketplace wanted to know what they would get even before they went out to buy anything. We began to structure our expectations about products around stability and predictability.

Welcome to the age of "branding"!

Producers realized that their future success was tied to branding − a response to the new consumer and the new global marketplace.

A brand can be conceived as a formula:

Brand Equation

$$BRAND = \frac{\text{tangible attributes} + \text{intangible attributes}}{\text{price}}$$

Value Equation

$$VALUE = \frac{\text{tangible attributes} + \text{intangible attributes}}{\text{price}}$$

BRAND = VALUE

All manufacturers and product developers know this.

Developing a brand as an embodiment of a product is today the only way to structure product development in a global marketplace. You cannot predict fashion, or style. You cannot anticipate visual consistency or taste. As we all know, success in the marketplace is achieving the "tipping point" but, there appears no way of predicting the content of that tipping point.

However, you can create in the consumer marketplace some anticipation of what "you get" in a product line. You do this through hitching products to values, to feelings, to anticipations, to expectations...in short, to consumer predictions and expectations. A brand allows a consumer to defy disappointment or confusion by giving people predictability.

Brand is the conjunction of innovation with predictability. It allows one to defy change with stability. Brand allows the consumer to graft onto a consumer artifact, – whether it's a purse, a pen, a shoe, a car, an iPod, a BlackBerry – a constant measure of value. The specific artifact may vary, but the value attributes remain constant.

Cultural anthropology teaches us that one of the most important features of all cultures is totemism. Totemism is that sense of knowing, or familiarity, or recognition between a person and an object. The person absorbs the attributes of the object. The person believes in the attributes of the product, not its functionality.

Consumers absorb the values of the product. You absorb

it and it becomes part of you and your personality. The running shoe is not simply to run on, not just an object defined by its functionality, but rather a public statement as to who you are, how you project yourself to the world. It allows a short-hand for others to recognize who you are. So much of the consumer world today is totemic in its character. Indeed, much of branding recognizes the very core of totemism as a defining feature of the global consumer age.

Seasons may come and go; they may vary from one year to the next. Ages come and go, prosperity is succeeded by disaster. But what ensures the stability of society is the constancy of totemism. What stays constant are the values that people absorb and impute to their artifacts, ensuring stability, consistency and predictability.

We invest very heavily in this aspect of the consumer society — by absorbing brands and brand/totemic objects, we attempt to defy change, trauma, disappointment, anxiety. We can absorb value by bonding with a brand. Our material objects define our personality. By making a brand choice, you assume the personality of the object. It becomes you, you become it.

When a person decides to buy an "Apple" or a BlackBerry, they are not just making a consumer choice based on functionality, they are making a totemic decision. They begin to define themselves, their personality, and their creative intent through that choice. They join the "tribe" of Apple as opposed to Microsoft and other alternatives. That is the power of the

Apple brand or any brand. You become part of a global consumer tribe, recognized by others, bonded to your likeness with others.

The French have an expression, "Je suis Renault" or "Je suis Peugeot" – I am Renault or I am Peugeot. This is an example of bonding with a product, or a product branding itself on to and within consumers. There is a totemic association between the product and the consumer.

There is a substantial paradox or irony, of course, in the age of branding.

Marketing is always a force for change. Fighting change may be a lost cause. Embracing change, we are told, is what one must do. There is a severe price one pays for the obsession with change because change alone may cause dislocation, trauma on a personal level, on a corporate level and on a marketing level. By connecting with the brand, consumers can adopt changing products. Brand gives reassurance for artifacts to change.

Changing the name of a car every few years is an "iffy" matter as is changing the name of the model too frequently. Mercedes does not change its name; rather it changes the number for its new models. American cars, by contrast, are "repositioned" in the marketplace with new names and new models, rather than new numbers.

There seems to be an apparent contradiction here. Consumers do demand and expect "newness" in products, or at least, it appeared that way with the American automobile makers, until recently. Yet, they also want to be able to recognize a product and gain familiarity with it.

One must seek to balance the pervasiveness of change with a sense of familiarity with product. To achieve this, one must find some stability and predictability within the context of change. In the global consumer society and marketplace, brand attributes are the chosen way to resolve this paradox or irony.

The purpose of branding is to reduce confusion. Its objective is to create trust between the consumer and the product. Branding is all about creating this trust.

There are numerous elements in branding — brand recognition, brand management, brand image, brand identity, brand personality, and brand promise.

One can ask simply why and how do we select consumer products? The answer, superficially, is to satisfy a need. To satisfy a need, you need a motivation. So, how do you create this need? Or how do you affect the need? Needs can be either material needs, but in this 21st century, there is significant emotional need. The motivation is intricately tied to the emotional need. This "need" compels you to THE product, the brand. It becomes emotional.

So...how to create this emotional need? You do so by creating a feeling, almost a myth, and a bond between the consumer and the product or product line. It is recreating a totemic association — I am "Nike" or "Cartier"...I am "Renault" or "VW"...I am "Toyota" or "Honda"...I am "Apple" or "BlackBerry," etc.

In the world of branding, corporate names are key. You

may change the names of the models, in cars or computers, but the presence of the corporate name with its identity assures you that you can trust the product because the product is branded!

In turn, branding means that the corporation has endowed or imbued its products with certain values regardless of the model or the changes that it has made. Trust is the key. There is no second-guessing between the consumer and the product, or between the product and the manufacturer. The corporate name delivers the promise. The consumer feels close to the product because they know it; they have confidence in it. Both the product and the consumer have recognition. They expect not to be disappointed.

This emotional link reduces the complexity of choice... it makes it easy...it gives you belief...a structure of anticipation...a diagnostic of how...why...what to feel, what to think, what to know.

Branding is constructive. To brand something or to create a brand, you need to make a promise and deliver on that promise. Any promise must be surrounded by values and it is these values that drive behaviour.

A successful brand creates a personality, and every product emerging from that brand is imbued with that personality. The personality of the brand is based on the values. The values are built on an expectation of rewards to be accrued from that brand. The rewards are built on the functional benefits that, in turn, are based on the attributes.

We can visualize the notion of brand as shown in the Brand Bull's Eye figure.

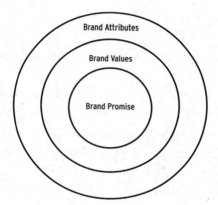

chapter six

Beyond Branding...Affinity

"You have to think differently in order to do things differently."

Branding is thought to be the elixir of success in the marketplace today. But, we also see that brands do undergo serious erosion and almost trauma. The promise that GM made to its customers was almost completely eroded by the end of 2009. Distrust had replaced trust. Disbelief had replaced belief. Disappointment had replaced confidence. The global fascination with the recall crisis experienced by Toyota in early 2010 also tested the resilience of the Toyota brand.

It is worthwhile asking, Is there something beyond brand which can bind or bond a consumer to a product? What do successful brands do? How do you create brands that "step out" of the ordinary? In the marketplace today, so cluttered with products, brands, messages, what is the point of differentiation? How can you differentiate your product from others? How can you keep ahead of the others? How do resilient brands withstand or overcome stress and trauma?

The nature of leadership is that leaders create followers.

To lead, you have to be followed. In politics, there is the notion that great leaders provoke in people a sense of devotion, a desire to follow, a sense of attachment, almost a magical capacity to bond people to a leader. This is often treated as charisma...an intangible quality, rarely observed, that seems to be possessed by some leaders. They have an inner capacity, an almost magnetic attraction, that provokes loyalty, faith, following, belief, commitment – and even more!

The "more" must be thought of as having the force of a covenant. It is not just an agreement, or a contract, but a connectedness that has almost magical or even quasi-religious power. It is based on a powerful belief, a conviction in the correctness of the choice or the bond between the leader and the follower.

In the marketplace, the concept of affinity is like charisma; it's the attachment people have to products or brands. A combination of the tangible and also intangible assets provokes this affinity in people. Affinity means to be connected to and with; it is the lasting ingredient of association; it is the epoxy, the crazy glue between a person and a product. Branding is a deliberate attempt to create relationship and recognition between a product and a person, or between a brand and a crowd. But affinity is what keeps that relationship tight, lasting and enduring. Affinity is the charisma of leadership in the marketplace. It is the force of attraction.

Affinity endows people with a sense of intimacy, a deep

sharing, a proximity and attachment to a product. It is almost a moral category where people invest heavily in following, being attached to, being connected with. They have faith and belief!

Think of chemistry…chemical affinity happens when dissimilar chemical species end up forming chemical compounds, when that which is different comes together to form a conjunction, a union, where atoms aggregate or bond.

Can this happen in the marketplace? How is it that people come to attach themselves to a product or a brand in this almost "chemical" manner?

They do so, for sure. But how? Under what conditions? Can we know the process? Can we deliberately provoke or can we engineer this notion of affinity?

Today, this is the real challenge of market research. We know and have learned the tools of branding. But can we uncover the magic of affinity in the marketplace?

It is often remarked that in this day and age of virtual reality, the plethora of communications and messages, in the age of multitasking, the one key ingredient of human experience that is becoming more and more scarce is our attention. Branding used to be about provoking awareness in people. It involved knowing or knowledge of the product.

There is another complication in branding today. People can know quickly and easily. They can know not just by experience, but the "Googlized" world makes knowing more accessible, easier, more thorough and more instantaneous.

Knowledge is a very widely shared commodity today and it's becoming increasingly accessible. So, how is success in the marketplace affected by the Googlization of knowledge?

Optimism is an aspect of culture, it is a value, and it is a way of doing something. Optimism is all about expecting success. But optimism is also part of a larger triangulation of experience. Throughout life, we learn many lessons and many of the lessons of life we learn through the educational experience, an experience that is now globally practised. Socialization, of course, teaches us many lessons necessary for the viability of society. But formalized education in a structured environment also teaches us many lessons beyond their specified content.

Pyramid of Success

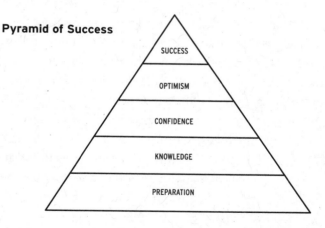

The pyramid of success starts with preparation. In undertaking any task, you must be prepared. Every student knows that if you want to do well in an examination you must be prepared. You must spend time, a valuable commodity, to get ready, to think, to absorb, to structure your thoughts and to focus. Without preparation, you may take a "flyer" or give it a "shot" in the hope of success. But the chances of success are limited. Preparation is at the base of the triangulation of success.

With adequate preparation you acquire knowledge. Knowing is familiarity, getting into things, exploring in depth, recognizing the road-map of how ideas, thoughts, facts, and evidence intersect and are related to each other. Knowledge is familiarity with the details and the big picture simultaneously. It is the zoom-in and the zoom-out of the "Google map" – the close-up and the far-out perspective. It takes time, discipline, and is premised on preparation.

With an adequate knowledge base, you gain confidence. Confidence is not bravado. It is not the feeling of superiority or invincibility. It is not based on faith or hope. Rather, it is part of a process, a slow, deliberate, structured process, beginning in preparation and moving upwards to knowledge.

Confidence provokes optimism. Optimism is planned behaviour. You become optimistic about a result of an action only if you have adequate preparation, you have gained sufficient knowledge and you have acquired confidence to achieve a result. Optimism is the upper reaches of the pyramid of success.

Optimism is an active and dynamic concept. Optimists,

whether they are people, companies, countries or politi-cians, act and take responsibility for becoming informed and for making decisions. Optimists see failure as change-able and are motivated to take actions that lead to success. They are deeply familiar with the process of the pyramid of success. That is why they seem so self-assured. They are willing to invest in the time, energy, and discipline required to reach the upper levels of the pyramid of success. That is why they are able to provoke a sense of security. They appre-ciate that success emerges from optimism because it is planned behaviour.

Success is not based on the roll of the dice, or hope, faith or whatever. Success is the result of discipline, a mov-ing up the pyramid process: preparation, knowledge, confidence, and optimism lead to success.

The "Toyota Way"

Companies create an internal culture that affects the way they approach the marketplace. Perhaps one of the best examples of this internal culture, until very recently, has been Toyota. The current revelations of Toyota's problems indicate not that the internal culture, built up over many generations of practice, is defective, but rather that there was a betrayal of that culture. Culture is a way of doing things based on values. In their haste to become the world's largest automobile manufacturer, Toyota allowed other concerns to subvert their own values and internal culture. Their public apologies have reaffirmed their own commitment to return to that culture and to re-embrace their values.

Toyota created the "Toyota Way," a deliberately planned set of structured behaviours. This is predicated on two very important Japanese principles: *kaizen* and *genchi genbutsu*. These are the core values for the corporation, their standards of behaviour. *Kaizen* is a planned process of structured behaviour. It formally builds on previous learning by using a teamwork structure to improve performance for the final product. *Kaizen* is an optimistic process because it is about preparation and discipline, and it encourages dynamism, flexibility and curiosity.

In addition, Toyota practises *genchi genbutsu*. The essence of this value is going to the source to find the facts needed to make right decisions, build consensus and achieve goals as quickly as possible.

Toyota talks to and listens to everybody to get a full perspective on an issue. It arms itself with knowledge – this is the only way to meet the future with confidence and a higher degree of certainty that the strategies implemented will succeed. Toyota takes all the time required to plan fully, but once a decision is taken, it is able to act quickly and decisively.

These two guiding principles drive optimism for a corporation like Toyota. They give Toyota its personality. When Toyota introduces a new product, like the hybrid vehicle, the Toyota Way makes them confident and optimistic that they will succeed. They have no doubts. The Toyota Way is planned behaviour engineered to achieve optimism and drive to success.

The personality of Toyota is intrinsically tied to quality. It took many, many years and decades to build this global personality, but they did so. Some might argue that Toyota is "boring," but they consistently deliver outstanding quality. Some might say that Toyota's designs are staid or boring but Toyota would not allow a designer to execute a shape, whether it is a rear-light assembly or a fender, that compromises the quality of that feature.

For example, we did research and compared Ford's Taurus rear-light assembly to Toyota's. The Taurus light assembly had almost triple the number of welds. The question to ask, obviously, is, Which one would leak first? The answer is clear: the one with more welds. Toyota would not allow its designers the freedom to design a product that would require that many welds. In a company like Toyota, quality supersedes design.

The corporate culture of Ford trucks was also rigid and disciplined, based on preparation, knowledge and optimism. They always believed that the next generation of Ford trucks would be better. "Ford Tough" was not just a promise, but a way of life, the definition of the corporate culture. It was also a design and build imperative. They knew they would succeed. In the corporate culture of Ford, the Ford truck guys always did their own thing and got what they needed to drive their success.

The corporate culture of Ford cars was different. There was a lack of discipline. Everybody had an opinion. There was no consistency in their approach. They changed the names of cars, not just models. Ford car people were endlessly anxious about their products, their models, and they were anxious about the likelihood of success.

Over the past few years, there has been a concerted effort to change the corporate culture of Ford cars. With coherent leadership and a recommitment to quality and frugality Ford cars are reasserting their place in the global competition of vehicles.

Just knowing a product or recognizing a product is not sufficient any longer. There is a growing predisposition in people towards cynicism. There has been too much disappointment in the marketplace. Too much has been promised and too little delivered. There is too much turmoil and instability.

It is becoming more severe. Active and aggressive critics are rampant and seem to be present everywhere. It is a function of being able to communicate easily and effectively. Opinions are no longer mediated by the media. Everybody has instantaneous and easy access to the media of communications through social networks and the Internet.

With the rampant presence of disappointment, whether it is in products long trusted such as the Big Three in the

American auto industry, or the integrity of Wall Street, or the collapse of the mortgage market, and even disappointment in Toyota, everywhere confidence is diminishing.

In this 21st-century environment, it is now crucial to provoke different feelings in people, conjoining people's emotions to the brand or the product. Recognition used to be sufficient for brand success. But today, that is no longer. Success now lies in connectivity, in provoking affinity between the brand and the customer.

Building Affinity

The dichotomy between knowing (a rational process) and loving (an inner emotional experience) is becoming more pronounced in the marketplace. Consumers rationally use their desktop computers, but they love their Macs – that's true affinity. To succeed, one must not only build the pyramid of knowledge but also the experience of affinity. One must find the appropriate balance between identification and enthusiasm, between knowing and loving.

Today, we get to know a lot and very quickly. Access to knowledge in the marketplace is easy, detailed and very quick. When in doubt – Google! When you want to know – check it out! What do others think? No problem…all the information is there. If you want to know what to purchase, find out other people's experience with the product. Googlized information is everywhere – quick, easy, cheap, and comparative. You can make up your "own mind" based on everything out there. You don't simply trust what you've been told; you check it out with your friends, with people like you, on Facebook, Twitter, etc.

The result is that we are very well informed. And, we are also more cynical and skeptical. Don't believe what you see...don't believe advertising...don't believe very much. We live in a supersaturated world of marketing, branding, advertising, PR, messaging...and more.

So, how does one make a consumer decision? And how does one influence a consumer decision?

Think consumer, think purchaser, think emotion, think senses...think affinity.

Affinity is the way to restore both credibility and personality between the consumer and the product. Affinity goes back to the truths of cultural anthropology. Affinity is all about culture and the way we live; about the artifacts around us and how we feel or associate with them; it is the reconnection between business and the street, between the story-teller and the listener. There must be cultural relevance and emotional connectedness.

Brands come and go and try to recreate themselves. What good brands do is attach themselves and propagate values that are enduring. Therefore, they can outlast the many economic cycles or demographic cycles that are part of social transformations. Good brands are like people: they have a story to tell. They start with the brand promise. The promise is like an indelible personality. It is like the sense children have about their grandmothers. It is there. It does not change. It is constant, recognizable. It makes you feel good. It is enduring.

Toyota had a personality inscribed in its conjunction with quality. Apple has a personality inscribed in its design, its association with youth and creativity. They have their own, unique story, told again and again so that the consumer knows what to expect.

But beyond brand lies affinity. How does a product acquire emotional relevance and character? How does a product tap into the enduring feature of a culture or of a great story – meaning and truth – so that people want to hear the story again and again, so they want to go back to the product year after year, hear the message again and again and then are even willing to retell that message to others?

Affinity implies this long-term relationship.

The collective consensus is the genius of the marketplace. It is this collective consensus that defines success or failure. There is a deep wisdom and intelligence in how people behave in the marketplace. Often, it appears that they can be fooled. But this wisdom, this collective consensus, emerges again and again and produces results.

What affinity means is that there is also an emotive consensus in the marketplace that underpins this intelligence and wisdom. That is what charisma means...that the emotive consensus draws people to leaders, creates leaders and crowds. This is what remains endlessly fascinating about politics – the leader as attractor, the leader as a creator of crowds, followers. Doubt, hesitancy, evaluation, knowledge…yes…but their success is epitomized by their capacity to engender this emotive consensus.

The lessons can be projected into the marketplace. Today, products that will endure, that may outlive the cycles of brand prominence, are the ones that achieve this affinity.

The remaining questions are, How to engineer affinity? Can it be engineered?

Affinity today is predicated on telling a story, an effective story, about a brand that has integrity. You cannot lie to people; you cannot deceive people. The collective wisdom in the marketplace today works at lightning speed. Fraud is exposed very quickly. In addition, affinity is predicated on a brand where optimism is built into and engineered into the very DNA of the product line.

Brands today, to achieve affinity, need to define their personality. The elements of personality are tied to how you tell a story, how people feel in relation to that personality. Today, you relate to a product through its personality as it is exposed through its storied quality. And like grandmothers, products must have enduring character!

Brands are like people. They all have a story to tell. And, we as consumers or listeners or observers get attracted to some stories and not to others. Good stories are credible, provoke attachment, and engender feelings of proximity.

People are attracted by personality, that unique "je ne sais quoi," that peculiar combination of external appearance and internal character. This is what affinity is.

An interesting example of brand affinity is Apple. Apple understands its customers and delivers products that appeal to their sensibilities and their intuitions. Apple products do not always dominate the marketplace. Indeed, in many product categories, they are relatively small. But there is an affinity that links their consumers or loyalists to their products. Apple users feel they are part of an exclusive community; they become members of a tribe. They have a stake in the brand. They internalize their loyalty to the brand. They relate to their products in an aesthetic, not just in a functional, way. The succession of innovative products from Apple, the iPhone, and now the iPad, continue to affirm the affinity between the consumer and the product line.

People often "wish" for something. What is a wish? It is an act of the imagination where the person envisages themselves inside a picture, a product, a scene, a relationship, etc. Of course, a wish can be provoked by envy, or hope, and it often is. But "wishing" is very much an aspect of human motivation and today, the power of products can trigger the imagination of people into wishing for their acquisition or experience of that product. That is what also triggers affinity. A public's imagination gets fired up with a desire to get connected or linked to that product. "I wish I had an Apple, I wish I had a Porsche, I wish I had...etc"

Affinity is the act of realizing the wish, of linking the product and the person, of realizing the envy or hope, or it is the culmination, fruition and realization of the act of imagination. That is why affinity is "beyond" material reality.

Affinity is about creating a "community" or a "communion" between the product users and the product producers. Or, affinity is about creating a tacit covenant between the consumers and the brand — a covenant that defies functionality and geography and outlives product change. That is why affinity is beyond branding. It is stepping out of the ordinary into the next stage of consumer consciousness and pushing the frontiers of this global consumer consciousness.

part two

Stories from
the Marketplace

chapter seven

Wonderbra

In the world of market research, there are many ways to gain insight, or to secure understanding. Although there are several standard ways to do this, very often it is valuable to pursue other avenues for insight. And, often enough, looking at the unusual yields astonishing results.

Here is the story — a true story. A market research story.

Larry Nadler was the CEO of a small and successful "foundation garment" manufacturer in Montreal, Canada. The company was called Wonderbra.

Larry and I would meet regularly on Sundays in his office in Montreal. I learned about the company as we discussed his problems. He became familiar with how I thought, the kind of research that I was doing. Over a brief period of time, a deep sense of mutual respect evolved. Larry bought into my language and into my desire to find a way to move his company to the next level.

This was in the late 1960s and early 1970s. The Women's Movement was in full swing. Many women were trying to redefine their role in society. There was, of course, the sexual revolution, but there was also a revolution about how people felt about themselves. A major element of it expressed itself in how people dressed. The outward appearance of people reflected deep personal aspirations, sentiments and feelings.

San Francisco became very important. Everybody was well aware that the epicentre of this revolution was in California and specifically in San Francisco. Popular culture was undergoing profound transformation there and its repercussions were felt everywhere.

I approached Larry to fund a study — surprisingly — of women's attitudes towards nudity. I wanted to know what people thought and, more specifically, what women's attitudes were towards women's underwear in this epicentre of the sexual revolution. If Larry's company was to move forward, if undergarments were to make the leap into the new and emerging culture, we had better know something about women's attitudes to sexuality and undergarments.

I concluded that doing survey research would not yield meaningful results. Instead, I decided that I should conduct interviews. But where? I suggested that some answers or insights might be found in the topless bars and restaurants in San Francisco. I wanted to interview both men and women, because women, not just men, did go to topless bars and restaurants. Why were they there? What did they see? What did they think? Did they identify with the dancers? How? Why?

It became clear from my interviews that men and

women had the same view about women's bodies. They both wanted women to look good and they wanted women to care about the shape they were in. After spending a few more days talking to young people in Haight Ashbury, San Francisco, I realized that what was defining the movement was a preoccupation with appearance and a deep concern for a sense of freedom.

Freedom meant many things, and for some women freedom meant they didn't want to wear a bra at all. By abandoning undergarments they were rejecting one of the constraints that society was imposing on them. Other women were less brave. They wanted to wear underwear that was flimsy, sheer and light. Freedom meant wearing less, showing more, abandoning constraints, being more overt! We now found the key to take a concept into the marketplace.

We wrote a report that changed Wonderbra's entire approach in designing, manufacturing and marketing women's underwear. They stopped making foundation garments and girdles. They designed, produced and marketed Dicey – sheer, light underwear. They wanted to crack the market for first-time bra wearers and young teens who wanted to feel free and open, but who were not ready to wear clothes without a bra.

"Dicey" became a signature new brand for Wonderbra. Dicey fulfilled the aspirations of the movement because it delivered a no-bra bra. Brilliantly packaged, the new sheer bra was sold in a little, well-designed box that looked like a dice cube. At that time, this was risky proposition, but it succeeded because it captured the changing value structure of the time. The new bra design, the story told in a great advertising campaign and the packaging all worked well because the client understood that their previous product lines had to be left behind. The new product lines tapped into the evolving and changing culture. Our research assisted them in understanding that new culture, and they were willing to take that creative leap. They developed a new product and were able to communicate the new product through imaginative advertising and unique story-telling. It caught on, it did change the "shape" women were in and it led in the marketplace for many, many years.

The new bras allowed women to feel they were on the edge, even though they were wearing something. But it felt like and looked like they were wearing nothing. Perception is reality, in an obvious way. And that was the truth for the perception of both women and men. The new bras were a statement of new attitudes, about who women were and where they were living. The old concept was that a bra was a foundation garment built for comfort. Most women didn't need that comfort.

The new bra concept was that women's breasts were showcases. They were attractors. Eye tests had shown that when men look at women they first look at their breasts, and then their faces. That was reality in the new age. No shame, no inhibitions. By showcasing the breast in the new bra, women were making a statement about their personalities; they were reinventing how they felt, how they related to the world. They were making a statement about their freedom. Wonderbra captured all this: in wearing as little as possible, women were able to display the "goods" and to redefine themselves. The new bra became an expression of intent, of values, of personality. It made an iconoclasmic statement.

Wonderbra, taking our insights from nude bars and restaurants in San Francisco, recreated themselves as a manufacturing and marketing company. They redefined a product. They became a leader. They created a following. The process was not just of branding a product and a company, but rather it was affinity because they created a product that connected with society's emerging attitudes.

In the marketplace there are leaders and followers. Wonderbra became the leader and, of course, because of their success, there were imitators. Their success was that an entire generation of people, women and men, could communicate with others by identifying with the phrase "we care about the shape you're in." They recognized and associated themselves with the freedom that the Dicey product allowed and showcased. This creative leap not only redefined what Wonderbra manufactured, but also redefined the working environment of the company itself. The staff felt good about working for Wonderbra because they were living in and creating a new world. Through Wonderbra and the new world, new customers were created.

The message of Wonderbra was the message of the times. This way of thinking about freedom, bras, about people themselves, became internalized, and captured the essence of the attitudes of the day. It became the signature expression in their advertising. All the Wonderbra commercials, all the stories the advertising told, all proclaimed that Wonderbra "cared about the shape you're in"!

Brilliant advertising is always through story-telling and repetition. Advertising basically functions because of effective story-telling. A good story is always worth repeating…and repeating…and repeating. We learn this lesson very early in life – in all cultures. When you read or tell a young child a story, you know the story works when the child says "again." You may get tired of reading or telling the story, but if the story is good, the child wants repetition and continues to ask for it "again" and "again," countless times. It works. It marks the child, it has impact. It affects the memory!

Great advertising is great story-telling because it captures the values and the mood of the day. In so doing, people look for repetition; they do not tire of it. They remember and enjoy. The message of Wonderbra – *we care about the shape you're in* – was that message for that time. And, it lasted as an iconic brand for two decades. The message still reverberates today because it is lodged in memory.

Effective story-telling based upon a quality product introduced into the marketplace through a unique look and package worked. Advertising created affinity for the Wonderbra brand. Women were drawn to Wonderbra, they associated themselves with the new look, the feel, the image, the experience. Wonderbra assumed a charismatic role in the industry. It became a leader and others, the competitors, followed this lead. The marketplace responded and in so doing an entire industry was transformed. This is what affinity does...it captures the value structure of a time, transforms product lines, creates leadership and followers, transforms behaviour and redefines an aspect of our culture. Wonderbra became a major North American company. Larry Nadler eventually sold his company to Consolidated Foods.

Almost every consumer product can be understood as an artifact of a culture. Thus, by looking around, by studying these artifacts creatively we can get a clue to the culture. Artifacts are not just utilitarian. Yes, many serve functions. But artifacts are also loaded with content, emotion, statement, feelings. Our study, which started in a Montreal factory and then in the strip clubs of San Francisco, gave us an insight into how to "read" an artifact, the bra, in a different way.

The creative leap was taken by the company, our client, in redesigning, redefining and manufacturing a new product to fit the times! They successfully took a concept – freedom for the shape you're in – and made it stick in society! They created a new artifact for a new time, consistent with a new sensibility that was quickly emerging in society.

Insight can be engendered from surprising sources.

Good market researchers seek out any vein from which to mine insight. Good clients are risk-takers willing to make that "creative leap." The story of Wonderbra is one such example.

chapter eight

The World of Diamonds
A Potlatch Strategy

It is somewhat ironic that the world's largest and most powerful diamond company, De Beers, would engage a Canadian consultant to conduct some major research for them in the 1980s. At that time, it wasn't known that by the year 2010 Canadian diamonds would have the largest market share in the global trade of diamonds. But marketing and market research is full of coincidences and surprises.

Diamonds occupy a special place in many cultures. They are peculiarly important artifacts.

Everybody, or almost everybody, wants to brag about something. Everybody wants to feel good, and one of the ways in which we make ourselves feel good is by having material possessions. Diamonds are a particularly visible artifact and tend to be taken out on special occasions for public display. Diamonds allow one to brag, to show others that you have something that is important, that lasts forever and gives you status. Like most artifacts in any culture, they are endowed with both overt and covert meaning.

My De Beers story is about taking an idea, or a series of

ideas, and infusing those ideas into society. The success of the product and the success of the marketing effort was totally dependent on a redefinition of what diamonds meant in society – on an idea and a series of insights that we uncovered by research.

What is so special about a diamond? What does this artifact tell us about a culture? What does it mean?

On one level, diamonds are symbolic of commitments. One gives a diamond to symbolize a commitment of one person to another in the hope that it will last. A diamond is supposed to last forever. It is endowed with meaning because it is enduring, hard, it sparkles, and it is transparent. Giving a diamond indicates the enduring quality of that commitment.

Also, the bigger the diamond the more you demonstrate your affection and love for the person to whom you give the diamond. You spend once, but there is an enduring aspect to that act. It is an act of extravagance not practicality, but it has enduring consequences.

Diamonds tell a story. But they are also embedded with memories. They carry silent memories to be shared quietly and privately.

The pioneering work on defining diamonds as cultural artifacts was done by the Ayers Agency in 1933. They gave diamonds the attributes that "diamonds are forever." They successfully made the diamond a symbol of permanence and associated the vows of marriage with the giving of a diamond. That totemic association of marriage with a diamond was then absorbed by most cultures and survives today.

In 1987, I was approached by De Beers Consolidated Mines to conduct a study. There were three objectives for this study: first, to prove or disprove ten hypotheses about the implications of various cultural, sociological, psychological and behavioural trends on the present and future diamond market; second, to develop insight into certain other specific aspects of diamond retailing – the importance of credit, and the importance of design; third, to develop a set of marketing recommendations for De Beers.

The first hypothesis examined was "values attributed to luxury items in adulthood have roots deeply tied to childhood." The research showed this to be correct. People who were given diamonds as children have a much more positive attitude towards diamonds than does the average person.

The second hypothesis was "the acceptability of and need for diamonds may be linked to an individual's level of self-esteem." The results showed that there is an almost linear relation between one's liking of diamonds and one's level of self-esteem.

Hypothesis three was "diamonds are social glue which identify and maintain interpersonal relationships." This hypothesis also tested positively in the sense that love is the primary message that a diamond transmits to both men and women; to the person who wears a diamond and to the person who sees it being worn; to both the giver and receiver of the diamond gift.

The fourth hypothesis was "diamonds play a role as a mouthpiece or communicator in society." Our research showed that while the pure or aesthetic value of diamonds is important, their communicative powers are also significant. For women, they communicate an emotional message. For men, in addition to the message of love, there is another message: a diamond worn by the woman the man is with is a symbol of success.

Hypothesis five stated that "diamonds can transform personal events into milestones and should be associated with traditional lifestyle occasions." The research showed that a diamond gift makes the occasion on which it is given a totally memorable occasion. Pieces of jewellery, particularly jewellery containing precious jewels, are the most memorable gift people give or receive.

The sixth hypothesis was that "consumers are receptive to relating diamonds to life cycle events and willing to extend the number of these events." The results of the research showed this to be correct, particularly with respect to a girl's 16th birthday party, the 10th wedding anniversary and a woman's 50th birthday.

Hypothsis number seven was "Americans are willing to pay for size, not clarity; thus, a 'secret society' approach to selling quality might have potential."

The notion of a "secret society" evokes an anthropological perspective, namely, that there are some aspects of life, important aspects, which are known to only some elements of the society. That is what a witch doctor does in certain societies. Only they have access to these secrets. Yet, many people want to know those secrets.

In the case of the purchasing and the giving of diamonds, there are secrets associated with the item. In diamonds, there are four "Cs" that define their value: clarity, cut, cleanliness and carat. These secrets are known to the purchaser and the giver. These secrets may be shared with others. But they may not be. The cult of "diamonds" is surrounded by this element of secrecy and that is part of what makes diamonds a most unusual artifact in so many cultures. To this day, the entire world of diamonds, from source to processing to selling to giving to marketing, is still surrounded by this element of secrecy and cult.

The data confirmed that, to an American, size is the most important attribute of a diamond. However, clarity was almost as important as size. The secret society hypothesis was not proven conclusively but the quality of the diamond is very important, suggesting that for some market segments, a marketing strategy based on quality could be effective.

The eighth hypothesis stated that "given the existing social climate, the outlook for the diamond market is favourable. Particular attention should be paid to second-tier baby-boomers, the 'tail end' and the over-50 generation."

The data showed clearly that owning good jewellery, particularly diamond jewellery, is gaining in status in American society. For this and other reasons, the outlook for the diamond market was favourable.

Nine stated "men need to learn and must continue to understand the importance of diamonds for women." The research showed that men understood reasonably well how a woman felt when she wore diamonds, but more education of men in this area was needed if they were fully to understand what a diamond means to a woman.

Ten stated that "self-purchase as a motivator should be explored." The conclusion from the research was that while the thrust of marketing efforts should remain "the gift of love," it was found that self-purchase should be targeted towards career women, members of two-income households and divorced women.

Diamonds as cultural artifacts led us to one of the core concepts of anthropology. And, here we found "potlatch." We took this concept and reframed it into a strategy.

Our strategy for De Beers was to suggest to them a new orientation, a new idea — the concept of the diamond potlatch. It was based on anthropological concepts, sociological realities and popular perceptions of the intrinsic qualities of diamonds.

We proposed the impregnation into North American culture of a diamond potlatch through the establishment of customs whereby life cycles and life-stage events must be acknowledged and celebrated with the exchange of the diamond gift.

Potlatch was the custom, the public venue, where acts of generosity and the giving of gifts was sanctified as an aspect of culture. Potlatch marked a significant event in the life cycle of people. It also, in the anthropological sense, involved the public display of wealth in a festive context. It was particularly well known and associated with West Coast indigenous peoples. It engaged everybody, usually the family and the entire community. It was related to the stages of one's life. For example, a potlatch or ceremony related to births, rites of passage, weddings, namings and honouring the deceased.

Our recommendation was that diamond potlatch become part of our culture's rites of passage. By transferring an anthropological concept into a marketing concept, we defined a vehicle to sell more diamonds.

We identified five major diamond potlatch occasions: the 16th birthday, without question, was an appropriate life-cycle occasion. The engagement event was a second occasion for the purchase of a symbol of commitment, the diamond. The third occasion was the marriage. The fourth was the celebration of ten years of marriage and marked the celebration of the end of the "marriage roller coaster," when the couple could now look towards the future with assurance of a secure and lasting life together. The fifth was the celebration of the 50th birthday and the purchase or the giving of a diamond to both men and women was an act of recognition not only of age but also of their enduring sex appeal.

The idea of diamond potlatch was based on promoting life-stage events as a vehicle to sell more diamonds. Betrothal was only one life-stage event. By adding other life-stage events and by enacting the potlatch diamond strategy, a new marketing initiative was created. The insight emerged from the research we did for our client. But it was also based on taking an anthropological perspective and using it to appreciate and understand contemporary culture. The diamond as an artifact of culture that could be renewed again and again throughout the stages of life provided new marketing opportunities to the client. By layering insight over values and by appreciating that values drive behaviour, we were able to provide our client with a marketing "edge."

De Beers took our recommendations and developed an advertising and marketing strategy that was brilliant. They told the "story" of diamonds and its meanings through the life stages whereby the story touched people emotionally. By appreciating the nature of potlatch in our culture and its various life stages, De Beers was able to weave the magic of the "diamonds are forever" story into a reinvigorated marketing strategy.

Diamonds as cultural artifacts now permeate many, many cultures. The totemic meaning of diamonds is almost global and the commercial success of this product in many societies and cultures is premised on the refrain that "diamonds are forever" and are wedded to potlatch occasions. The insights derived from cultural anthropology reinterpreted the meaning of this commodity and product in the consumer world.

chapter nine

The Ford Truck Story

‑ ‑ ‑ ‑ ‑ ‑ ‑ ‑ ‑ ‑ ‑

Part 1: Ford Tough

"Built Ford Tough." Everybody knows that motto. It was the signature, the hallmark of the Ford truck brand. It has survived since 1979. It etched itself into the brand and into the way people perceive Ford trucks.

Advertising works because of effective story-telling. Brilliant advertising works through repetition of effective story-telling. Great advertising works because it tells a story, repeated again and again, that captures the values and mood of the day.

For decades Ford told the story of "Built Ford Tough." The story was about how tough their trucks were. The stories allowed viewers and readers to place themselves in those stories because they were about real people with similar hopes and dreams. The stories provoked an association between people and what they saw. The images provoked not only identification between the viewer and what they viewed, but also a deep desire to imitate what they saw.

"Built Ford Tough" was the way Ford defined a way of thinking that people not only saw, recognized and associated with, but it was also the way people could have affinity with the product. Beyond the brand lay this affinity, that deep sense of recognition and attraction. By purchasing a Ford truck you not only had a functional vehicle but you also bought into a way of life that defined you as a person. The person became attached to and associated with the personality of the tough truck. Ford effectively created an affinity between the person and the object or the artifact. By buying the tough truck you also become totemically associated with all the personality characteristics and traits of the object. The integration of person and object was complete – affinity was achieved!

The power of "Built Ford Tough" became the brand promise. The Ford truck people, from engineers to management, from designers to finance people, everybody at Ford truck took this brand promise seriously. They all knew what they had to do to keep quality and the brand promise alive and successful. They recognized they could not compromise on toughness and quality.

They told the story of "Built Ford Tough" over and over, again and again. They did this for more than thirty years. They recognized that they had to prove to each generation, each cohort of potential truck buyers, that Ford would deliver on its brand promise.

The stories they told through their advertising did

change in terms of nuance and background. But the message always remained the same. Tough work, tough environments, strength, pulling boats, working in rough terrain, doing tough things whether it was at work or play (and both were important), regardless of the environment, from farm to construction, from mountains to deserts, from city to shoreline, Ford tough would always deliver.

Affinity made Ford trucks so successful that it allowed them to be the number one selling vehicle in North America. The endless advertising campaigns brilliantly executed over a long period of time assured the success of the vehicle and cemented the relationship between the consumer and the brand.

Our culture admires people who can do tough things. Tough trucks – Ford trucks – defined a person in terms of his or her mental toughness, their work lives and their personal lives. Toughness is a hallmark of the American value system and values compel behaviour. The messages from Ford trucks that created affinity were tied up with the value system of the culture – freedom, the outdoors, ruggedness, overcoming the odds, delivering the goods, reliability.

This message, the story, has lasted for many, many years. Its durability and its longevity are tied up with the affinity between the consumer and the product. Ford succeeded in developing a lasting "covenant" between the marketplace and the truck consumer.

Part 2: Quality is Job #1

While Ford had achieved a dominant position as the number one truck manufacturer in North America, at the same time its automobile/car business was suffering from dismal sales results.

Research showed that consumers were very skeptical about the quality of Ford cars. *Consumer Reports* made it obvious to buyers that there were deficiencies in the Ford auto product. There were two ways to address the problem. One could, of course, change the product and improve its quality over a long period of time. That would involve engineering, manufacturing and assembly changes and much more. The other was to find out how to address the marketing question. How to convey to the consumer and the public that Ford was serious about the quality issue?

We did research for Ford that tried to address the latter question. Advertising is about story-telling, story-telling that is effective and convincing.

Ford had tried an advertising campaign that used professional actors to try to convince the consumer that they did care about quality. However, our research suggested that the campaign could be much more successful and convincing using real people. There was a belief in America that people working on an assembly line did not care about the quality of the products they were building. There was a belief that these workers were on drugs or they were the dregs of society and that was why they ended up working on the assembly line. Because they were not committed to the product, they could not build quality products.

Our recommendations were that if Ford were to succeed, they had to convince Americans that the people on the assembly line were no different than the people watching the ads on TV. We had to assure them that assembly-line workers in Ford plants looked like them, dressed like them and thought like them. The proximity of the viewer to the product, mediated by the assembly-line worker whom they could recognize and trust would assure the public that they could trust Ford and the quality of the products.

We convinced Ford to go to their assembly lines and abandon the actors. We convinced them to show real people in the commercials. But further, we convinced them that they should identify these workers by their names and identify the plants and assembly lines on which they worked.

By convincing Americans that people on the assembly line were nice folks, hard-working, that their intentions in the workplace were honourable, that they were committed to quality and trying their best to build better products, they succeeded in convincing the consumer and the general public that their Ford products were better quality.

Good advertising is good story-telling. The advertising and the story told in the advertising campaigns motivated management to deliver quality and, also, it convinced the public at large that Ford — the people and the brand — was very serious about quality. Ford wanted to and would deliver better-quality vehicles.

This changed the perception of Ford. People began to believe that Ford quality was, indeed, better quality. The campaign of "Quality is Job #1" lasted some twelve years.

Then, some years after the campaign was launched, somebody convinced management that quality was now a "given" and it was no longer necessary to be advertised or communicated. This story-telling stopped and the advertising changed! No repetition. No conviction!

It took another number of years, but the perception of Ford quality deteriorated because they stopped the story-telling of Ford quality through advertising. Management forgot it was the core of the brand – Job 1! The message stopped. The public was detached from the original story. Their memory faded quickly and their faith in the product declined severely.

The perception of a decline of quality hurt Ford significantly, so much so that today Ford is back to advertising quality. It is always important to remind the public, to sustain the public belief and faith that quality is important to Ford. They must deliver quality products. Quality is not a given. Quality must be earned with the product itself, with the experience of the product, but also people must be reminded that quality exists. Quality is not just a slogan, it must be seen to be a commitment – an enduring value that is recognized by the public and is also the motivating character of the producer. It is built into every product, every product line. It is the life-blood of all aspects of the company and its products. Only then can it be convincing to the public.

Remember that Toyota took many years and decades to come to dominate the North American market. It did so because it built its reputation and its entire corporate strategy on superior quality. People believed Toyota because it aligned itself with a value system, a value system that was more credible than Ford. People had faith in Toyota quality. They had affinity with the brand of Toyota. Quality was fixed into the DNA of a Toyota product.

It is intriguing that Toyota has recently moved away from quality and is positioning itself as "moving forward." What does that mean? It appears that Toyota, with the global concerns about the environment, is trying to reposition itself as a world leader in environmental issues. But the quality question came back to haunt them in 2010 with a vengeance. They must now reassert and also prove to an increasingly skeptical public that quality remains in the DNA of the company and its products.

Will it succeed? Early indications are that it will be difficult. Why? Because quality is always the cornerstone of success in the global competition of products. People today have knowledge. Through Google and other social networking channels, product information about price and quality is communicated easily and quickly. Those products that align themselves with quality succeed. If you forget this simple truth, if you forget to tell the story about quality, if the DNA of a product leaves quality out, it will suffer in the marketplace.

Part 3: Redefining a Product Category - The Story of SUVs

The record of Ford is quite intriguing. And no more so than the fact that in the last decades of the 20th century this company introduced two concepts that changed the entire auto world in North America. Their success in North America spawned many imitators in Europe and in products coming from Japan and Korea.

The story is told in two parts – first, personal use trucks and second, SUVs, sports utility vehicles. These two ideas created enormous wealth and success for Ford and they changed the entire automobile industry.

In reality, these two major innovations were based on an existing product, the Ford Ranger truck. But what happened transformed and recreated a truck, the Ford Ranger, into something totally different and unique. One of the elements that drove this transformation was research we conducted.

It was the 1970s. Ford retained us and they wanted to understand why Ford Ranger sales were falling. The Toyota truck product had hit North America and was eating significantly into Ford truck sales.

Where to start? How?

Thursday nights, in Los Angeles on Van Nuys Boulevard, young men would cruise the area in their tripped-up trucks. We decided that we should go to this site and figure out what was happening. We set up a trailer there to observe and interview these young people.

What did we learn? What did they tell us? These young people were customizing their Ford Ranger trucks to make them into personal use vehicles. They were painting their vehicles, they were taking out the seats and putting in leather seats, they were upgrading the sound system and they were using the bed of the truck for fun, for sex, for sleeping, for excitement! Trucks were no longer work vehicles. They were being transformed into something else.

Even more, they were taking these vehicles off the road, driving them through deserts, up hills, off normal roadways, through canyons and more! All of this was to increase their enjoyment, to differentiate themselves from other pick-up truck owners. Their trucks had nothing to do with work vehicles. Their vehicles, configured differently and customized, were for fun. Their vehicles were personal use vehicles, for excitement, exploration, adventure and also, but only incidentally, for work.

We also learned that these pick-up trucks, designed and sold as work vehicles, were, in fact, cheaper than cars. Young people were buying these less-expensive vehicles and investing their time and money in customizing them and fixing them up to become fun vehicles. In the different California landscapes – mountains, deserts, seashores, cities, suburbs – these vehicles reflected their lifestyles. They had effectively transformed a truck into a user-friendly, personal-use vehicle oriented to pleasure and not a workplace vehicle.

We developed the concept of "personal use trucks." While they may have started out as trucks, these vehicles were painted differently and made to look like fashion vehicles, both on the outside and also on the inside. On the inside, the interiors were dramatically upgraded with better seats, better sound systems and more comfort. On the outside, they were individualized with new paint, new patterns and new colours.

We recognized that this specific public group had developed a new way of thinking about an existing vehicle. It was not the designers and the engineers who had developed a new product category. Rather, our research revealed that something special was already taking place in the marketplace!

Our observations on the site on Van Nuys Boulevard forced us to understand how these young people were redefining the very concept of their "vehicles." We learned that the current marketplace for vehicles did not provide them with what they really wanted. So, they creatively reconfigured an existing vehicle to suit their own values and needs. Once we understood this, we then shared our findings with the Ford truck designers, product planners and engineers. The result of this process of insight, recognition and analysis then led to design, product development and engineering that developed the first personal use truck and ultimately the SUV.

Personal use trucks started with the Ranger and then were extended to the F-Series, first the F-150 and then on up. A personal use truck made the cabin comfortable — it made it possible for the truck to be the family vehicle. Cabins evolved to have back seats and premium sound systems — all the comfort features!

The Explorer SUV was simply a Ranger product designed to meet the playful needs of younger people and younger families. It didn't take a huge investment in new technology to create it. The Explorer evolved from and was inspired by the personal use Ranger. It was built off the Ranger platform and shared many of the same interior features.

In time the SUV too evolved, and bigger and more luxurious SUVs were built off the F-150 platform. The pick-up truck had been transformed into a luxury vehicle! While work trucks remained very much part of the Ford truck story, the creation of these new vehicles — personal use trucks and SUVs — grew trucks into a larger and more profitable category.

The new values we recognized in our research — work, recreation, fun and utility — all combined into one vehicle, provided the basis for the SUV. Ford recognized that new products had to be developed to satisfy these new values.

The new SUVs would be used to transport families, to do family activities, to go camping. These new SUVs became the all-purpose vehicles that suited the new lifestyle of Americans. They moved stuff with it, they took vacations with it, and they went off road with it. These SUVs made people feel good about themselves. They reinforced their individuality and allowed them to have fun; they gave them a sense of their own personality.

These two concepts, a sports utility vehicle and the personal use truck were the main successes of Ford in the 1980s and 1990s. By taking an existing product, recognizing the intuitive transformations already taking place in these products in the marketplace by young people, and by boldly recreating two derivative products, Ford brought major innovation to the entire automobile industry.

Marketing is a force for change. Ford recognized something and changed the way vehicles were made and marketed. Now, in SUVs and personal use trucks, Americans felt great. They were sitting higher up than in other vehicles; it was called command sitting. You could see the road. You felt stronger and you were more in control. You were youthful; you were having fun.

These vehicles carried the industry for the next twenty years. Their success inspired or influenced almost every other manufacturer to create their own model of the SUV. This is a perfect example of leadership, as leadership can be defined as the ability to create followers.

This innovation in the industry was not technically driven; it was marketing driven. It recognized a new understanding about how society was changing. The clue was Thursday nights on Van Nuys Boulevard in LA and watching and understanding what young people were doing. And why? It was taking an existing product and adjusting it to society's wishes. It was listening to what people had to say about the way they wanted to live and how they used their vehicles and the choices they were making.

The image of the vehicle both on the outside and on the inside became the image and the self-image of the person who drove the vehicle. These new vehicles helped people feel very American, proud to be American, because this was an American innovation. By taking the F-series pick-up trucks and remaking them into personal use vehicles and even luxury vehicles you changed the marketplace. The industry and the personality of the vehicle driver were changed. The new vehicles reflected significant changes in the American value system.

If you understand values of a culture and the emerging values, you can influence behaviour. Marketing is a force for change. The new product was aligned and reflected the new value system emerging in America at the end of the 20th century. The Ford brand was able to capture and reflect those new values.

The advertising of the SUV told a wonderful new story in the chapter of the evolution of the American way of life, its lifestyle. It confirmed for everybody that we could become reattached to the environment, to the outdoors; we could participate in the adventure of exploration, in the saga of American innovation, in a new way of feeling good.

The new lifestyle, defined by the SUV, became embedded in the American psyche. And everybody who wanted to could participate by purchasing an SUV — even if you lived in the city.

The SUV reflected a new American personality and a new value system, and it deeply affected human behaviour. People, through their SUVs, made a statement about who they were, how they were acting, how they were conscious of a new lifestyle. The new culture defined by the SUV went outdoors and everybody wanted to be current, up-to-date, even if you lived in an urban situation. SUVs tapped into this shift in our culture. Not having an SUV meant that you were out-of-date, not in tune with the evolving culture. That culture went outdoors; it was participatory, healthy, active and environmentally conscious. There was a new consciousness of life evolving in the marketplace. And, the SUV as a vehicle and as a cultural artifact confirmed this shift. The marketplace was redefined, a vehicle was recreated and a new lifestyle was confirmed.

The success of these vehicles was due to affinity. People were attached to these new vehicles not simply because they performed a function, but because they recognized something in these products that made them feel something about themselves, about their society and their value system, about that to which they aspired.

Affinity is also related to the desire to "wish" for something, that intangible that compels human behaviour in many circumstances. By acquiring the "it," there is almost a wish-fulfillment stage that we do not give up easily. It captures our imagination, it makes us part of that object, we are "in it" and being "in it" and part of it becomes deeply satisfying on many levels.

Affinity confirms reality, affinity is intrinsic to self-perception, and affinity became the glue between the product and the public. That is why these new types of vehicles succeeded for so long. That explains their durability. And, that is why so many other automobile manufacturers around the world, recognizing the fundamental character of this value shift and the affinity between these types of vehicles and the new lifestyles, have imitated them.

chapter ten

The Pinto Story
Knowing Your Weakness...Telling the Truth

"Advertising is always a function of the product's expression
of itself. Fallibility and vulnerability may be positives."

The folklore about Pinto is that it was the car built by Ford
that exploded!

Yes...some cars have indelible reputations. Pinto is the
car that exploded if it was hit in a collision from the rear.

This was the late 1960s. Most cars in the 1960s had
problems. It was the era of the big automobile but was also
the era where all automakers realized that they had to build
smaller cars. Everybody was working on a new subcompact. For GM, it was the Vega. For American Motors, it was
the Gremlin. Ford had its own answer.

Ford launched the Pinto as a subcompact into the North
American market on September 11, 1970. The Pinto remained in the market through the 1980 model year. Within
four years after launch, the Pinto was in trouble. Articles
and news stories appeared portraying the car as more prone
to fires than any other car of the time.

The reputation of the Pinto as an unsafe, troubled car was hurting Ford sales in general, tarnishing their reputation. An unsafe car became the albatross for all Ford vehicles. Ford knew that they had to address the issue, but they also knew that they had to keep the Pinto on the market for another few years while they developed a replacement product.

How to address the issue and resolve the problem? Advertising, heavy advertising is one way to try to convince the public. Ford developed a series of elaborate advertising campaigns on how they were committed to solving the Pinto problem. They used spokespersons who were well known to increase their credibility in the public's eyes. Their campaigns had an aggressive edge to them, a hard sell, almost a shrill tone.

Our research for Ford at the time came to a different conclusion. We learned that "screaming" at the public about the problem, coupled with aggressive advertising only made things worse. People were not convinced. Advertising is communication. But behind advertising must be the recognition of a value structure. Values help fashion human behaviour.

Our research further showed that the public still had a great deal of goodwill towards Ford. They wanted to believe Ford. It was one of the Big Three. It had a long and reputable track record. Ford owned a huge part of the market, the second largest part. It was an old company and was becoming a global company.

How to address the problem and yet differentiate the problem with Pinto from the fundamental goodwill that the public had for Ford? That was the question.

The solution to the problem from a technical point of view was not that difficult. The "fix" for the Pinto problem was not complicated. It could be solved by putting a curve in the filler pipe leading to the gas tank so that the fumes from the fill-up would not back out when pumping gas into the car. This was a complete technical and inexpensive solution to the Pinto problem. Installing this curved pipe would mean that Pinto was not an explosive car.

We were asked to do some research on how to address the market issue – how to communicate this solution to a technical problem in a way that was credible and would restore confidence in Ford products?

We advocated a simple, low-keyed advertising campaign that did nothing more or less than to identify the fix or solution. This could be done with a simple diagrammatic explanation. The curved pipe would be installed in all Pintos – an inexpensive solution, a simple explanation... problem solved.

Our research and our recommendations were based on our understanding of the relationship between Ford and the average American consumer. People wanted Ford to succeed. They did not want to see Ford fail. They did not want to mistrust Ford. They didn't want to be aggressively advertised at.

Ford had to re-establish that basic trust between the

consumer and the product and the product and the company. They could do so best first by not denying but admitting the problem. We recommended that Ford start with a direct, simple, low-key statement and explanation, one that everybody could understand – "We will fix it." We thought that the credibility of the Ford brand could be restored. No great fanfare, no aggressive talk, no denial.

While we believed that we had the correct solution developed through our research, we still had to convince the Ford executives that this was the right approach. We still had to have access to the senior executives to influence them to accept the recommendations based on our research. Solutions to problems may be found, but implementation requires access and influence. Fortunately, we did have that access.

By explaining the problem and the solution to the public in the simplest manner, Ford succeeded in sustaining the basic trust with the public they had established over many decades in the marketplace.

With the solution, Ford was able to continue selling Pintos for some further years until they could introduce a new model in this product category.

In the marketplace the consumer is all that counts. Aggressive communications through advertising may well highlight and exacerbate the problem, rather than address the solution. In the marketplace, you cannot avoid the obvious. You cannot lie for very long and get away with it. Ford had to acknowledge the problem of the exploding Pinto. It could not deny it. It had to find a solution. It did so. It had to believe that the trust between the company and the consumer, mediated by the product, a "fixed" product, could be sustained.

One of the intriguing lessons from this story is that for Ford, admitting fallibility and admitting vulnerability, even as large a corporation as Ford, created affinity. People could relate to an apparent monster corporation recognizing that mistakes do happen. But what recreates the human face of the corporation, what restores confidence and affirms the proximity, the affinity between the company and its products and the consumers in the marketplace, is the element of fallibility and admitting such. This lesson is now considered the appropriate and classic approach to product failures – one that Tylenol successfully emulated in 1982 but one that Toyota did not, to its ultimate pain, in 2009 and 2010.

Affinity is the ability to tell the truth, exposing your own weaknesses, admitting error. By being fallible, even vulnerable, you create trust. Trust is a function of truthfulness. While "big" may encourage the sense of the powerful, fallibility may make for a more humane recognition and, as a consequence, may create affinity.

The lessons of fallibility and vulnerability as an aspect of affinity can be extended into other areas. Obama was successful in creating affinity to his leadership aspirations by playing out and recognizing his own vulnerabilities. People could feel close to Pierre Trudeau when his marital problems became public and when he faced them publicly with dignity and grace. Being too big, without a human face, may create alienation while being too small may create irrelevance. Products in the marketplace must find that right portrait, at the right time, in order to remain relevant and successful. The Pinto story is one such episode of a brand and a product on the verge of huge failure that was restored.

chapter eleven

Touch Zones
The Sensuality of Choice

*"Success is the result of preparation mixed
into the recognition of an opportunity. You win or lose
in opportunity situations quite quickly."*

One of the many conundrums in the marketplace is how do people make choices – do they know first or do they like first? Knowing vs. liking, what comes first? Another way of asking the question is, What makes one emotionally attached to a product?

Many people buy cars without knowing a great deal about them. They buy them because they look or feel good. Therefore, liking is more important than knowing for these people.

Impressions and first impressions have a major impact on consumer choice. One of the first and probably most important consumer choices people make is the purchase of their home. The second most important consumer decision relates to the purchase of an automobile.

Impressions happen very quickly. People look at book covers, for example, for between three to five seconds and then turn to the back cover. They gain a powerful first impression of the product – are they interested enough to look at the back cover? If they do, the entire process takes approximately fifteen seconds. They make quick decisions to purchase or not to.

In the 1980s Ford was going through a difficult period. Market share was falling. People were rejecting Ford products. Ford had done a major and very extensive research study. Among the things they discovered was that many people were coming to their dealers but they were not buying vehicles. There were many reasons. We were asked to do some follow-up research related to the conundrum of choice. We were interested in how impressions affect consumer choice in cars. More specifically, we were interested in very immediate or first impressions – how immediate experience could affect human behaviour.

The senses are our immediate entry into a product, or the first contact with a product. Design clearly affects how we "see" a product. But we are also tactile creatures. We gain a sense of a product, very often, by touching it. How does it feel? We are also audio-sensitive. How does the sound of a product affect our impressions of it? These aspects of our senses in relation to consumers' experience of vehicles were of considerable interest to us.

Based on our research, we developed a concept we called "touch zones."

We observed people's first relationship to vehicles. They

approach the vehicle and they begin to "sense" the vehicle by what we came to call the ten touch zones. In addition to these ten touch zones, our research indicated that people experience these touch zones in a surprisingly short period of time – 90 seconds!

This first encounter with the touch zones has a major impact on their impressions and evaluations of the vehicle. They come to an evaluation of the vehicle in a surprisingly short period of time based upon their contact with the touch zones. If these touch zones impress the consumer, they would be more predisposed to buying the vehicle. If they did not impress, the opportunity was lost.

In our marketplace, the success of a product depends on opportunities. If an opportunity is lost on a consumer, there is a high likelihood of failure. The touch zones start with the experience of getting into the vehicle. The first encounter is with the door handle. Sound and feeling…it had to sound and it had to feel precise.

Second, once inside, it was the steering wheel. It had to be thick enough so that people sensed security and if it was wrapped in leather, it had to feel firm but soft. The sensuality and peculiarity of feel – communicating security and both firmness and softness.

Third, the seat fabric. It had to feel smooth yet it also had to feel like it could last forever.

Fourth, the gearshift lever. It had to fit in the palm of one's hand, yet feel soft.

Next, the glove compartment. It had to open easily but in closing, the lock had to sound and feel precise.

Then, the door of the glove compartment had to be stiff, sturdy and firm. It could not be flimsy.

Seventh, the instrument cluster. The holes and sections had to be in the right place, visually appealing, and easily accessible to the eye. For example, we tested a Thunderbird where the tachometer was placed on the passenger's side. Most people felt that this was an insult to the driver.

Eight, the plastics, ubiquitous in cars now, had to feel right. When you tapped the plastic with your fingernails it had to feel and sound soft but also sturdy. We tested an Escort and one woman said to me when looking at the plastic: "The plastic looks like it is sweating!" It looked cheap and provoked negative sentiments. It gave people a sense that it was not good enough for Ford. Confronted by this finding, Ford changed the plastic prior to the launch of the product.

Back outside, the trunk. It had to open easily but when shutting the trunk, people didn't want to slam it shut. It had to move easily, up and down.

The tenth touch zone was the hood. It should open easily, the lever had to be easily accessible and it should close by simply releasing it. People did not want to slam the hood shut.

The 10 touch zones created an important impression on people. If they gave people a sense that this was a good-quality product, they were positively predisposed to purchase. If these touch zones gave a negative impression, purchase was unlikely.

People acquired a "sense" of a product by encounters with its touch zones. Sensuality communicates value. Choice in the marketplace has a lot to do with the dimensions of sensuality. Touching, feeling and sensing created impressions and defined predispositions.

Our advice to Ford was to make these touch zones exceptional in their vehicles and in so doing they would enhance the sensuality of choice. Limited investment dollars became more available to improve and enhance touch zones versus other aspects of the vehicle. The enhancement of sensuality created higher value in the vehicle. This would create at least the opportunity for purchase.

chapter twelve

Ford
Falling in Love and Out of
Love – A Story in Four Parts

Part 1: Falling in Love with Thunderbird

In 2000, at the Detroit Auto Show, Ford unveiled their concept car – the new Thunderbird. It was love at first sight! People were lining up to sign up so they could be one of the first to get one. People loved the new car – the concept, the mystique, the brand.

Demand so was high that when the car was launched in 2002 there was a waiting list and some dealers were able to charge more than $10,000 over sticker price. The potential for this car was enormous.

Why did Ford cease production of this Thunderbird after three years? Because "knowing" kicked in and once people got to know the car, they became dissatisfied. When they experienced the car, when they got to know it, they realized they had spent a lot of money for a car that didn't have fundamental features that they would have expected from competitive vehicles in the same or similar price range.

This Thunderbird didn't have automatic seat heaters, there was no GPS and it didn't have an automatic hard roof for the convertible. The fits and finishes were poor, especially the metal work. The gaps between the seams on the sheet metal in some cases were almost half an inch.

The car didn't deliver the expectation that people dreamed about. They fell in love but they quickly learned liking was not enough, and once they knew the product, rejection set in.

People clearly wanted this car. The brand history had created a mystery or ethos around the car. The public had a nostalgic and dream mythology about the original 1956 Thunderbird. The image of that car, the affinity for that car, the mystery, magic, the ethos surrounding that original car never waned. It became the dream American sports car.

The new Thunderbird delivered on looks but failed in so many other product areas. It was, unfortunately, a grab for profits without thinking about the disappointment that would result from an inadequate product experience.

The 21st-century Thunderbird is a classic story about what plagued the American auto industry and what really got it into trouble. The industry was producing a good-looking but inadequate car for the money. Quality was lost! The public recognized this and abandoned the product. People flocked to the competition because they knew that they were buying more quality for the same or less money.

Lexus was the competition and, in many respects, Lexus changed what was expected from the upper-mid-priced luxury vehicles. Lexus quality was second to none. It stressed pursuit of perfection and delivered touch zones that were impeccable. Moreover, Lexus was relentless in communicating quality and in delivering quality, both in the product and in service.

Thunderbird had affinity based on its heritage. There were memories of the original product, a yearning after that unique mystique that created the affinity in the public. Ford successfully capitalized on that affinity to launch the 2002 Thunderbird. Unfortunately, the product itself failed to deliver what people expected from a luxury vehicle, and so production was ceased after just three years.

Public judgment in the marketplace can be very, very harsh and final. The Thunderbird died! The lesson is that credibility is the key. People want to believe. They want to believe, truly believe. They believed in the Thunderbird. But, alas, performance is vital. You must deliver. If you do not deliver, credibility is gone and is irretrievable!

The further lesson, of course, is that a brand is a promise. It must deliver the promise. A promise cannot be a deception if the brand is to succeed. With Thunderbird, the look promised excitement. The brand promised high performance, a recovery of the successful experience embedded in the history of the vehicle. It did not deliver. The promise was betrayed by experience.

Part 2: Marketing Ploys & Designer Series

The designer series at Lincoln came out of qualitative research that we conducted for Ford. It revealed the power of exclusivity and the way to use "potlatch" as an inducement to consumer choices. People are attracted to being different and special. Lincoln was always an exclusive and up-scale product line for Ford. The challenge was how to develop a renewal of the product line to maximize sales?

The designer series was a series of Lincolns based on four world-renowned designers' reputations — Bill Blass, Cartier, Givenchy and Emilio Pucci. Launched in 1979, the Mark V Lincoln was unlike any other car. It had interiors and exterior colours designed by each of these world-class designers. They exuded extravagance, taste, uniqueness and were one-of-a-kind. They were different, they stood out, they shouted look at me! These cars sold for a huge premium. This series made a lot of money for Ford because it capitalized on a simple fact — people fell in love with exclusivity, extravagance!

The reality was different. There was hardly any difference between a Lincoln in the designer series and one not in the designer series. Mechanically, technologically, substantively, all Lincolns were the same.

This episode in the industry is an interesting example of powerful marketing. It was delivered by advertising executive Alan Levenstein of Kenyon & Eckhart. What is fascinating is that by putting a designer name on the vehicle and by giving it a unique colour, people were prepared to spend thousands of dollars more for the vehicle.

People with money like to be recognized; they like to be noticed. They like to be noted for their wealth, their style, anything which makes them "more than ordinary." The designer series was a perfect example of how to raise the price point and increase profitability in a product to take advantage of this urge to be noticed. Marketers still offer designer series today in everything from cars to child car seats!

Part 3: Double Discount

This begins with a simple story revealed by our research. The problem was how to induce more people to come to Mercury dealerships so that they could view the cars. There seemed to be a problem.

Our research revealed that there was a sense of fear when people approached dealerships. People were reluctant to enter a dealership because they thought they would be deceived and taken advantage of by the salespeople. They were totally anxiety-ridden about the prospect of visiting a dealer. So, many people would go to the dealerships on Sundays when the dealership was closed and inspect the vehicles.

We discovered that although they wanted to view the vehicles, they also decided at all costs to avoid meeting or speaking with salespeople. Sunday visiting was a solution – for many members of the public in the market for a car. Not for the dealers. Our research showed this to be a considerable problem in the industry. How to overcome this problem and to get people back to the dealerships when they were actually open?

Mercury developed what was called "double discount." The concept was simple and easy. On every car there was a sticker price affixed on the rear side window. The sticker price identified all the features of the car and the price. Mercury was discounting the vehicles but we suggested they use the term "double discount" to demonstrate value of the product in relation to the price. When people visited the dealerships on Sunday to avoid the salesperson, they could still be shopping actively for a vehicle because they had this discounted price visible to them. They felt very positive about getting a good perspective on the vehicle even without the initial intervention of the salesperson.

For the consumer, getting a good deal in the auto industry is still very important. Our double discount strategy didn't create a price war because there was no advertised price discount – it was part of the sticker price, was publicly visible and it could only be discovered at the dealership. It was an extremely successful strategy that helped Mercury sell many vehicles.

What is so interesting is that the entire marketing concept of double discount emerged from our ability to listen to people tell us that they did not want to go to dealerships because they disliked, or were afraid of, or could not relate to sales-people. They understood their own behaviour. They knew what they were doing. Their apparently peculiar behaviour was a credible solution to their own fears and dislikes.

People behaved in a certain way because they were driven by their values. Those values were honesty, integrity, transparency. They wanted to avoid anxiety, pressure, deceit, confrontation. They wanted to make a purchasing decision based on quiet consideration rather than high-pressure salesmanship.

We listened to what people were telling us. We trusted their own account and explanation of their behaviour. We then were able to appreciate what they said and turned it into a marketing opportunity and a marketing strategy.

Our research findings were then presented to our client, Mercury. They accepted our solution, and adjustment to sales and marketing was developed. The double discount strategy worked because it responded to people's values. It worked because it was transparent, clear and honest.

Part 4: Ride Tests and Ride Engineer

A little plaque in every Mercury Marquis read "Ride Engineered."

The purpose of the plaque was to differentiate the Mercury Marquis from its competitors in that product category in order, obviously, to boost sales. Mercury developed the whole strategy of cars that rode better and they developed a method of exposing a better ride by comparison testing with other vehicles, for example, Cadillac. But this point of differentiation, the Ford Motor Company claims, also had to be proven. That is why they developed a series of exceptional advertisements to prove their case.

How did they do this?

They would choose a route and drive the Mercury and the competitive vehicle over the same route. Then they would interview the respondents who sat in the back seat of the car and ask them a series of questions about the ride. The respondent would test two cars and ultimately evaluate which car rode better. Most of the tests took place on the West Coast.

How did the Mercury win almost every test against the competition? At certain speeds they would test one car against the other. For example, in one ride test they knew that at a particular speed the Cadillac would bottom out, meaning the car would hit a bump and you could feel it. On the same road and at the same speed the Mercury did not bottom out. People were asked which car rode better and, obviously, Mercury would win. The advertising agency chose different routes for the testing, but before a route was chosen it was tested to make sure the Mercury would win.

Mercury was tested against many cars, including Cadillac and Rolls-Royce, and Mercury would always win. Tests were carefully scrutinized by Ford lawyers. Questions were asked the same way for everybody.

The genius behind this marketing strategy was a fellow named Arnie Kusnetz at Kenyon & Eckhart. He was a brilliant, creative iconoclast with a wonderful sense of humour and zest for life. He demonstrated that Mercurys rode well under "certain" circumstances – that were pretested. All of this had nothing to do with a differentiated product.

The key was to understand the values Americans attached to "smoothness" of the ride in their cars. Americans wanted this sense because it gave them a feeling of luxury and also quality. A "ride-engineered" car tapped into these dual American values.

An entire and brilliant advertising campaign was developed around this claim by Mercury Marquis of being "ride engineered." One advertisement showed a diamond cutter sitting in the back of the Marquis. He sits ready to cut a very expensive diamond that requires absolute precision and skill. The tension mounts as he gets ready. The Marquis continues to drive on a street. Dramatically, he cuts it deliberately. The Marquis ride is so smooth, he is successful. Another brilliant advertisment showed a man dressed in a white suit sitting in the back of a Marquis. In front of him is a big plate of beef bourguignon. The man dips into the plate laden with dark wine sauce. He begins to eat the beef bourguignon. The ride is so smooth, he never spills anything on his white suit.

These brilliant stories told through advertising, told again and again, confirmed for the public that the Mercury

Marquis was, indeed, ride engineered. The stories affirmed values that Americans held dear to their hearts about cars. They wanted smoothness as a sign of solid, well-made cars, reflecting quality and the sense of luxury!

The diamond cutter and the man in a white suit eating beef bourguignon both evoked a sense of luxury and enforced the message that Marquis was different, special and excellent.

chapter thirteen

Ford and Corporate Culture

Taurus: A Detail

Taurus, introduced in 1986, was a car specifically developed by Ford at time when it needed a winner to stay alive.

The backdrop was that Ford had to establish itself as a producer of quality cars. It had to be proven that Ford would go the extra mile in order to ensure that its cars exuded quality. Taurus was the test case. The product leader in the development of the Taurus was Lou Veraldi, a veteran and experienced product planner at Ford.

Success in cars often is found in the details. Our previous experience with touch zones meant that we advocated devotion to details to ensure that people would be happy with the car.

We tested two gas-filled struts that secured the hood in an open or closed position. These would make it easy and safe to open the hood on the Taurus. They worked well. We recommended to Ford that they deliver a Taurus that was a touch above other Ford products. We wanted to ensure that there was perceived quality in this Ford product.

The corporate culture at that time at Ford meant that product planners could not, or should not, come in over budget on their products. If they came in on budget or under budget, they would be taken to lunch by the chairman of the company. This was one way of enforcing discipline in the company.

Taurus came in over budget because Mr. Veraldi fought for the struts to make an exceptional vehicle. Veraldi was convinced that he had to create a product that would surpass people's expectations of a car coming from a North American producer. He was committed to producing a quality product for the marketplace.

His determination enabled Taurus to succeed so much so that it saved Ford. He was not taken to lunch. He defied the corporate culture in order to create an exceptional product. Coming in on budget is not a guarantee of success.

Management does make a difference. It isn't just the numbers that count in product development. People need vision and they need to fight for what they think is right. You cannot satisfy the finance guys in a corporation at the expense of the consumer. If you diminish the quality of product, the consumer will find out and they will abandon the product.

In the marketplace the consumer reigns supreme. Consent is granted by the consumer to the product and its manufacturer based on an assessment of quality. If you abandon quality, you abandon the search for consent. Failure will result.

Mercury: The Failure of Differentiation

Ford tried to develop Mercury as a brand in the market-place. It tried to position Mercury as an up-scale, almost-luxury brand, in-between other Ford products and the luxury of Lincoln. It failed.

Mercury basically did not provide a different enough product from other Ford product lines. The design was different on the front end and it had minor trim differences. The brand failed because it could not deliver key product differentiation. The consumer was not prepared to accept Mercury as a better Ford, despite the advertising that Mercury presented over and over again. The truth about the product was transparent to all. The reality of the product denied the advertising claims.

This was the ultimate betrayal of the consumer. Ford Motor Company had to support its claim for product differentiation. But the consumer knew better. It was not a better product than other Fords.

All the advertising in the world, all the sophisticated communications could not deliver a credible story to the consumer. Mercury was neither a better-quality product nor a different product worthy of a higher price. All the advertising could not create affinity between consumer and product or brand.

Whereas Ford failed with Mercury, GM failed by having so many products, Chevrolet, Buick, Oldsmobile, Pontiac, claiming to be differentiated, each demanding consumer confidence and fidelity. But the reality was that the only difference between these products was in the sheet metal. Ultimately, the consumer did not respect GM. It continued to market cars on their claim for differentiation, but in reality this did not exist. The company, as we all know, drove itself to the point of bankruptcy. Today, both Ford and GM have moved to significantly fewer brands — but brands that are truly differentiated.

Consumers are very smart. They do get to know products in the marketplace. Sometimes it takes them time to catch up or catch on and to discern the truth. When they do, they have the power to reject and when that happens, companies suffer.

Companies must respect consumers' collective wisdom in the market. If they do not, if they believe that advertising can convince people regardless of the product itself, then they will suffer the consequences.

Today, GM is trying to reposition itself in the marketplace. They have had the chairman of the company address the public directly in some of their advertisements. In others, GM is asking the public to trust the quality of the product by at least giving GM products a try. This is one way in which GM is declaring its faith in the consumer and in the marketplace.

If you make a promise to the consumer, in today's competitive marketplace, you must deliver. Or fail. The marketplace ensures the supremacy of the consumer. And consumers always act in their own self-interest, regardless of what the advertising tells us.

The challenge facing advertising and advertisers today is that these more traditional media and forms of communication are up against the newer media, the Internet, social networks. People have alternative forms of information and these are extremely credible because they are unmediated. They are person-to-person. They have acquired enormous credibility, as well as spiralling use. The result is the enhanced empowerment and knowledge of the consumer.

chapter fourteen

Toyota
A Consistent Message That Got Through
- - - - - - - - - - - - - - - - - - -

Once upon a time there were the "Big Three"!

Then, slowly, ineluctably, unexpectedly, people began to listen to a message coming from a foreign source. The message was carried and verified by *Consumer Reports*, word of mouth, consistent advertising and marketing. The message was that Toyota meant quality. The assault on the Big Three lasted many years...but the story got through. We all know what happened.

Nobody believed that North Americans would not buy their "own" cars. Yet, the Toyota and Honda stories, and other car makers following in their footsteps, have proved that wrong.

Marketing can be a force for change. Advertising is spun around stories. It is the stories told that become the signature of brands. These stories create affinity, which results in loyalty and the commitments to brands. When a brand is developed with the consumer and becomes a trusted product that is delivered consistently over time, affinity becomes a reality. It pushes the brand to another level of reality. The product, the communicated promise and the imagery associated with the story-telling — when all these are combined, affinity is created and establishes the long-term, enduring relationship between people and that product.

The Toyota story — and the Toyota Way — is all about quality. This was the story told over and over again and confirmed by independent sources, such as Consumer Reports, J.D. Power and by word of mouth. The evidence became undeniable and overwhelming. Toyota delivered a quality product, better than the competition! This influenced consumer choice. Toyota became a winner!

The main reason for Toyota's success was that they trusted the people's judgment. The collective consensus makes wise choices. That is what democracy is all about and that is what the marketplace is all about. Toyota quality won the day.

In North America, Toyota won big against all the odds because they understood the power of quality and the importance of frugality to the consumer. They never compromised the product as is evidenced by year-after-year reports in consumer magazines. While this was taking place, the Big Three were losing focus. They claimed they were delivering variety with an endless stream of new models. But they always compromised on quality. Satisfying Wall Street rather than "Main Street" became the American way. Cost-cutting where it was believed that consumers would not notice did not work. Consumers noticed immediately. A collapse of quality and the use of cheaper materials became rampant. The consumer learned that the product got cheaper with each generation and they started looking elsewhere for quality.

After Corolla (the car for everybody) became a huge success with North American consumers because it delivered quality consistently together with frugality, came Lexus. At both ends of the price spectrum, the Big Three lost out. Quality triumphed. Toyota seemed to be invincible at all levels of the car market. The apparent invincibility of the Toyota brand was being delivered from the top to the bottom of the automobile market and everywhere across the globe. The appetite for global dominance took hold at Toyota.

Following success in America, Toyota was desperate to expand their penetration and to grow in the European market as well. Corolla was already successful in Europe. But they wanted to expand and sell more than one million cars. A "plus 5 percent" of the European market became a strategic objective. Yet, they recognized that there was resistance to Toyota, especially in Germany. And they also recognized that the old Corolla was staid, reliable, dependable, trustworthy, but uninspiring.

They developed and introduced a Corolla replacement. They wanted to make a statement with this new product. The German press wrote a lot about Toyota as the challenger to Volkswagen's dominance in Germany and its strength in the European market. Toyota believed that with a new car and a new name they would extend their enormous success and dominance from North America to Europe.

Toyota introduced the Aurus into Europe and tried to sell it as a brand "new" Toyota. Expectations were high. The press was very attentive. Customers flocked to the dealerships wanting to inspect the new Toyota. Toyota was expected to challenge Volkswagen in Europe with the new Toyota.

The reality was that the Aurus was a new shell but was based on the old Corolla. It had a new name, but it was not what the story said it was. As well, quality compromises had been made. It had cheaper plastic and rear seats that would not fold down fully. When Toyota tested the Aurus in Europe, they discovered that a very obscure and incidental feature caught many people's attention. People recognized that the turn-signal lights in this new car were not new. They were a carry-over from the Corolla. They also noticed that the engine was the old Corolla engine. They immediately looked at the new car and said that it was neither new nor good quality. Toyota had started cutting corners.

Consumers are very sensitive about little things in a product. It becomes their product, their valued possession. They have a right to be sensitive, to notice, to be on the alert for quality. Values drive behaviour and for the automotive industry, the values of quality and frugality are fundamental. One way to demonstrate both frugality and quality is by fuel efficiency.

Culture is a way of life. It is endemic to a society, to a group or community and to companies. The culture of Toyota is clearly spelled out in the book *The Toyota Way*. Every individual who comes to work at the company is introduced to the culture of Toyota through seminars and discussions and through the book. The culture is endemic to the delivery of the product lines. Everything is formulated, checked, rechecked and verified.

The two core values of Toyota, as demonstrated in *The Toyota Way*, are *kaizen* and *genchi genbutsu*, as mentioned earlier in this book. These values are about consistency and consistent improvement. They are built into the DNA of the company and all their product lines. It is this determination to consistently get better from generation to generation that has produced superior quality in Toyota products.

In the marketplace, the first objective is to create awareness. After awareness comes knowledge about the benefits of the product that might create interest. Marketing, building on the inherent culture and values demonstrated in a product, can create an attitude of optimism with individual products.

For instance, for 30 years, Ford told stories about the F series of trucks that relate to product toughness and toughness equated to reliability and dependability. These are the values that people began to absorb and to ascribe to themselves. The product, the Ford truck, allowed the consumer to experience their own personality and to connect to the way they think. They bought into quality. The message was consistent over time and the story-telling adjusted itself to the times. The core message of preparation, being tough, being able to do the job, never wavered. As a result, Ford continues to dominate the market in trucks. Consistency and consistent improvement creates a culture of optimism in the product. "Built Ford Tough" created optimism for the product itself.

Toyota did the same with the Corolla. People care deeply today about the efficiency of a car; fuel consumption is of considerable concern to all consumers. People equate efficient fuel economy with better quality. While efficiency is not a single issue motivator, it becomes part of the larger issue that is the quality of the total vehicle.

Corolla had superior mileage, demonstrating the value of frugality and efficiency and superior quality relative to the competition. It told that message again and again and it delivered over time. It created optimism about the product.

Indeed, optimism can even occur in the face of breakdowns. In the research we did about Toyota and Honda, where there were product breakdowns, the consumer often interpreted but also defended the breakdown as not something that you would expect from Toyota and Honda. The product was good, the breakdown was an anomaly. Regardless of the breakdown, people defended the product because of its quality. However, when we interviewed Ford,

GM or Chrysler owners with regard to breakdowns, these events were seen as anecdotes and to be expected: *Fix Or Repair Daily* (F.O.R.D.). While Toyota and Honda products are viewed optimistically and exude optimism, other vehicles are viewed pessimistically.

Many people think optimism is about hope, or hoping for the best. But we now know from medical research that optimism is a stage at the top of a triangle. First comes awareness, then knowledge, then confidence, then optimism and then success. If we apply this in a marketing context, as Toyota understood, you can create a culture of optimism. The first objective is to create awareness, and then it creates knowledge of the product. With knowledge comes confidence and the result of confidence is optimism.

Affinity preys off optimism. People have affinity to Toyota products because the products are imbued with optimism and they are so because there is a culture within the company that "injects" optimism in each of its products.

People are carefully watching the fate of Aurus in the European market. It is worth noting that Corolla still carried the Toyota brand in North America and the introduction of the new vehicle on the Corolla platform was marketed and seen as the next generation Corolla – evolution. This product met North American expectations. However, the experience of Aurus may well tarnish the very reputation of Toyota in Europe.

The tarnish on the Toyota brand globally has already

taken hold. Quality has, indeed, been compromised. The knowledgeable and empowered consumer has caught on and is severely punishing Toyota. The unforgiving public is wreaking vengeance on Toyota with Congressional inquiries, demands for apologies, by humbling the world's number one automobile maker. The "giant" is being slain.

The new head of Toyota, Mr. Toyoda, the grandson of the founder, has publicly recognized its problems. By placing the corporate objective of global volume above their stellar reputation for quality, he has admitted that Toyota customers and the Toyota brand had been compromised and betrayed. Quality and reliability, the two hallmark values of Toyota, must be restored.

Affinity, so hard fought for by Toyota over so many decades, is premised on transparency. The recognition of vulnerability and the acceptance of fallibility may be one way to assure affinity going forward. (Remember the Pinto example.) The case of the Toyota Way and the restoration of the Toyota Way are worth monitoring carefully.

chapter fifteen

Fear
The Gas Story

— — — — — — —

Heating during winter is a major part of the experience of those people who inhabit the northern hemisphere. For most of the last century, our choices were wood, coal, oil or gas. As the use of wood and coal faded by the 1970s, most people reverted to oil heating and had oil delivered to their homes by the oil truck. Oil home heating predominated until gas pipelines began to enter the market. Many cities and locations began to access gas as a viable and inexpensive alternative to oil heating.

Gas had a number of obvious advantages. It was cleaner, less expensive, didn't need delivery trucks, and provided a continuous, uninterrupted supply. It was also sold to the public as more efficient. The challenge to the predominance of oil was on – and it was a fierce struggle!

We were retained by the oil industry to examine the challenge and suggest some alternative response strategies. We conducted both quantitative and qualitative research. After a lot of research and many interviews, only one principle stood out, one perception was dominant in the mind of the public. It was simple, clear and unequivocal. There was an overt fear that gas could explode. People were fully aware of that fear; they expressed it.

Fear is a fundamental motivator for much of human behaviour, as are dreams. Once we discovered the dominance of fear and its direct association with gas, we had a clear lever to influence behaviour. By playing on that fear, one could induce people to trust oil! Fear is often expressed by anxiety. In our research we discovered both fear and anxiety. The whole idea was to capitalize on the deep and pervasive anxiety people had about gas. It may well be an irrational fear. Statistics may disprove it. Ad campaigns may attempt to deny it. But neither proof nor denial obviates the fear people had about gas exploding!

Fundamentally, we recognized a value embedded in our culture, a need for security, the absence of fear, and we were able to use this insight to market a product. We entitled our study "Gas Explodes!" We presented our study and its finding to some 30 or 40 oil executives, all members of the Oil Retailers Association. We put only two words on the overhead slides – *Gas Explodes!* Everybody got the message. It was crystal clear how to sell oil and beat gas in the marketplace.

Human behaviour can be motivated by fear. Fear often is expressed by anxieties. We discovered in our research both fear and anxiety. The whole idea was to capitalize on the deep and pervasive anxiety people had about gas. It may well be an irrational fear. Statistics may disprove it. Ad campaigns may attempt to deny it. But neither proof nor denial obviates the fear people had about gas exploding!

The industry now had a strategic and tactical approach to combat the encroachment of gas in the heating market. They ran an advertising campaign that was quite brilliant. It never said "Gas explodes." That would have been too provocative. Rather it showed a beaker filled with oil with a lit match over the beaker – a stark image with a very simple and powerful message! The demonstration was that oil does not explode and is also very difficult to ignite. Don't be afraid of oil! By extension, of course, it implicated the alternative – gas was explosive, dangerous, feared and unpredictable.

Advertising works best if the image and message are powerful, simple and effective. One could, of course, have argued for the competitive advantages of oil over gas – many words, many arguments. The oil industry understood that you could sell oil and reinforce its image based on what we had discovered in our research – people were overtly and intuitively afraid of gas exploding.

chapter sixteen

Livent
Price Points

The story of Livent is one of the most intriguing episodes in the entertainment industry in North America during the last two decades of the 20th century.

We all know that entertainment is big business. We also know that there are certain epicentres in the entertainment industry whose pre-eminent positions cannot be challenged – easily. In the film world, it is Hollywood. In the theatre and musical world, it is obviously New York and Broadway. Yet, over a period of two decades, one company starting from scratch, succeeded in making a dent in the predominance of New York. And that company was Livent.

We were retained by Livent because they had a number of problems. First, although they were selling out their shows for *Phantom of the Opera*, they were not making money. Was it possible to raise the price points for seats and not affect attendance?

We did a survey and three-quarters of the people who came to see the shows were coming for a special occasion, such as a birthday or anniversary for family members or friends. At the same time, we found out that these buyers wanted to buy the best seats possible to show that they were prepared to spend more money to mark these special occasions. Money was not a major deterrent. You did it for the person you were with. It was an expression of care and affection for the other.

We did not want to raise the price of all tickets to increase revenues. That would have been one solution, but a controversial one. Given that constraint, we had another solution to increase revenues. We recommended an alteration in the price points for the seats. We recommended that two-thirds of the house be sold as expensive seats. We then split the remaining one-third in half, with one-half being middle-priced seats and the other half cheaper seats.

Effectively, we did not raise the price on any single ticket of admission. And we could not reduce the price. All prices for all seats in the theatre remained the same —neither up nor down. But, based on our research, we recommended a reapportioning of ticket pricing within the theatre; that is, more seats were categorized as premium seats. We could raise the total revenue of each house performance. The new price structure increased revenue for Livent to eight million dollars — a significant sum for one show in one theatre in one city.

The second problem had to do with audience attendance. One of the reasons why New York theatre and musicals are successful is that they attract audiences from all over. New York theatre is a magnet, drawing attendance from far and wide. That was the secret of New York. But could it work for Livent in Toronto?

We immediately recognized that there was insufficient population base in Southern Ontario and the Greater Toronto Area to fill the Livent theatre night after night. We had to develop a strategy to get people from outside Toronto into Toronto to attend theatre. We did research in bordering cities in the United States, asking people whether they would come to Toronto to see theatre. We learned that people as far away as Pittsburgh would come to Toronto to see theatre. Among the many reasons why they would come was the reputation of Toronto as a safe, clean city, which made it preferable to dangerous New York. Our research allowed Livent to develop a concentric zone theory so that people within 100, 200 and 300 miles could choose different transportation packages by bus with a matching price structure, depending on where they lived.

Livent reaped the benefits of this larger population pool. People wanted to feel good about going to the theatre. Almost 60 per cent of the people attending *Phantom* were not from Toronto; they came from far and wide, up to 300 miles away, because the product was good, the price structure fair, and the transportation was organized and reasonable. They had their special occasion, their theatre, all at fair pricing. Toronto could now compete with New York.

What was important about our research was that it

tapped into people's feelings about themselves. Special occasions meant something to people. Theatre was one way to make it special and memorable, to themselves and to others. They also wanted to feel safe. Toronto made them feel safe. New York did not. They did not want to suffer anxiety. By building a predictable transportation component into the special occasion, which offered easy pick-up, delivery and drop-off, they were assured of no anxiety.

In this marketplace, bundling values became very important. First tickets and transportation, then hotels and meals...all of these were bundled into a predictable, safe, easy-to-use package. This was the marketing brilliance of Livent and assured their success. People wanted to feel good about their experiences. Going to the theatre the Livent way was a good experience, a full experience, a safe and predictable experience. You could enjoy it and you could tell your friends and family about it.

chapter seventeen

Guests Not Customers
The Four Seasons Hotel

— — — — — — — — — — — —

Values are guiding principles of behaviour. People have values. They need them. Corporations must also have values if they are to endure. These values must be inscribed in every facet of their operations. Efficiency is an operating principle. Values are more fundamental and must be inscribed not only in operations but in the people who work in corporations.

A good example of this is the Four Seasons Hotel. This hotel chain was developed on a set of principles and values established by Isadore Sharp. The principle of service quality defined what he wanted to do and he never wavered, even in tough times. He believed that a hotel was an environment, an experience, an ambiance. You create and reinforce this ambiance through a devotion to details. It was this devotion to detail that was the point of differentiation for the Four Seasons. It was built into the very corporate culture of the chain and it emanated from the very top, from Issy Sharp himself.

We did research for the Four Seasons on what customers expected from a luxury hotel chain. Issy Sharp had an intuitive understanding of what luxury people wanted. Our research bore this out and helped him develop a consistent story in the marketing of the Four Seasons Hotels.

Sharp understood that the brand promise of the Four Seasons was its consistency. In every one of the hotels in his chain, the guests could expect the same things. It started with the mattresses on the beds. They had to be the best that money could buy, better than you had in your own home. At the Four Seasons you were assured of a very good night's sleep. People recognized and appreciated this so much that the Four Seasons eventually sold their own line of mattresses.

Second, at every Four Seasons you could expect a local influence on the amenities in your room. In the UK, you could expect the best of British soaps; in Paris, the best of French soaps, etc. In every Four Seasons you would expect the very best brand name amenities that country and that culture could offer.

Third, the Four Seasons built its reputation on freshness and authenticity. There were always freshly cut flowers in the lobby and in each room.

Fourth, as a measure of recognition of place, there was always a display of antique china in each Four Seasons. Again, this was an aspect of the corporate culture of the chain.

Fifth, the Four Seasons understood that their guests felt most at home in a hotel of no more than three hundred rooms. Guests wanted personal attention, so the chain could never become too big, overcrowded or impersonal.

In a competitive environment, trust is absolutely vital.

This trust extends from the corporation to its product to the consumer, and also it extends to trust in staff. At the Four Seasons, staff had the freedom to make choices and if you had a question about something, even on your bill, management entrusted staff with authority to make it right, on the spot.

Recognition is a hallmark of friendliness. People want to be recognized and respected. At the Four Seasons, staff were trained to know their guests and they were the first ones to recognize the name of somebody who called from their room. This made people feel that the company cared about them personally and went out of their way to know them.

People go back to the same hotel in order to be recognized. They like to go back to the same restaurant to be recognized. This gives them a feeling of comfort. It is often remarked that students, and others, sit in the same seat in every class or meeting, even though they are not obliged to. Familiarity and recognition were built into the Four Seasons experience.

Understanding the value system of people allows one to understand their behaviour. The Four Seasons Hotel realized that wealthy people want to be recognized and noticed — they define themselves in certain ways because of their particular value system. The Four Seasons aligned itself with these values and they created an environment and an experience that mirrored those values. The consistency of the brand in delivering both familiarity and recognition ensured the loyalty of the Four Seasons guests. The hotel had a personality, a friendly personality, a caring personality. This led to affinity, a step beyond the brand!

chapter eighteen

Pulse
The Context of Listening and Observing

Human behaviour always takes place in a context. If you want to study human behaviour and understand it, you must appreciate that context. Good market research must be aware how that context influences decision-making. Cultural anthropology teaches us that to gain insight into human behaviour and to understand the complexity and meaning of any culture you must study the "sites" where people live, act, behave, interrelate.

The sites of market research may vary. It could be Van Nuys Boulevard in Los Angeles on Thursday nights, where we set up a trailer to watch, observe and interview the young people with their pick-up trucks as discussed earlier in this book. Other sites can be constructed or concocted, such as interview rooms. Over a number of years, we developed an alternative site for market research for Ford and we have used this model of a constructed site for a lot of our other market research.

In the 1970s, Ford was a very well-known brand, indeed, the only global brand of vehicle, but it was losing market share. The question was why? What was happening to Ford as it was facing competition from many manufacturers in the auto industry?

We were asked to figure out this problem and it seemed to us that doing interviews was not enough.

We came up with an alternative idea. Why not put all cars, Ford vehicles and competitors' vehicles in one large room or site? Then our idea was to have not only different cars but also different people at the same site. The different people would be Ford owners, Ford rejectors, prospects, or people looking to buy a car, the open-minded, owners of competitors' cars and more. We wanted to fabricate a "site" reflective of the marketplace – that is, a simulated marketplace, a constructed marketplace.

The objective was to observe and interview people in this facsimile or fabricated context, this recreated marketplace, in order to get people's first-hand, qualitative impressions of the various products. The idea was to create a site with a diversity of products and people, and study it as a reflection of the total marketplace.

We called it a Pulse, a unique kind of research. A Pulse is a series of concentrated focus groups occurring at one time and in one place, in a simulated marketplace. It is a way to understand the dynamics of the marketplace through gathering the right people and the right product mix into one single site.

The right people will be a cross-section of the marketplace, including some who own the sponsor's product and others who own competitors' products, as well as sales consultants and various people involved in the sales chain of that product category, advertising personnel and management.

To gain insight into the complexity of the marketplace and to find the right language that expressed the diversity of experience, impressions, attitudes of that marketplace, we also recruited other kinds of people. We invited people who had significant abilities to articulate ideas about their experiences with and impressions of these vehicles. We invited community leaders, psychologists, engineers, architects and others whose verbal skills could be helpful.

It was a "face-off" between Ford and other vehicles. The Ford products and competitors' products were set up side-by-side where people could observe, experience and assess the range of alternative products in one place. In the case of cars, it meant that thirty or so cars were in one large site so that owners, potential buyers and others could view and interact with this range of vehicles.

The purpose was to allow the researchers and also Ford management to observe customer interaction with the product and to listen to customers as they responded to the product they saw. Management, in this context, was given an immersion into customers' attitudes and behaviours.

Confronted by this variety of people and a variety of products all in one context, all in one site, we were able to study, listen to and attempt to understand the marketplace. We also included a variety of advertising items so we could assess the efficacy of ads and communication techniques.

In qualitative research such as a Pulse, people are very willing to tell you almost everything. People want to help you, to contribute to a solution to a problem, to tell you what they think, to articulate their impressions, to offer their opinions. People do open up in a Pulse to let you know how they feel, to engage in the story-telling relative to the products they confront or to the purchasing decisions they have made or are thinking of making. People willingly want to feel part of the big picture.

Pulse research can be done relative to the various segments of the marketplace. For instance, we have conducted Pulse research in Texas in order to understand the purchasing decisions of the Hispanic segment. It was clear that trucks were the preferred vehicle. The men and women both came to the purchasing situation. The men appeared to make the decision, but our research revealed that the women determined the parameters and limits of the budget, how much could be spent. If the salesperson did not speak with the woman, the sales opportunity was lost.

Another Pulse was done in New York City. Ford appeared to have a problem in selling Ford Motor Company products to the Jewish community. Ford thought that there was an historical basis to the problem, an association of Ford with a history of anti-Semitic sentiment. The purpose of our Pulse was to determine whether this was the case and to find a solution to the problem. Our conclusions, based on a New York Pulse, were that Jewish vehicle buyers did not have a bias against Ford for any anti-Semitic reasons, but rather that they did not buy Ford products because they thought that the product was poor quality. Neither historical memory nor religious bias was at play. Rather, the fundamental value that drove the purchasing behaviour of these consumers was their concern with quality. Jews who could afford them bought Mercedes products because they thought they were quality products.

The marketplace is, indeed, complex. But through market research one can gain an understanding as to how it works. In qualitative research, you can hear people's stories. You can find, develop or construct the appropriate sites and listen to these stories. And, in those stories lies the threads that define values, which are the guiding principles for behaviour.

Pulse research not only allowed people to confront various products in a simulated marketplace, but it also forced executives to face the competition. Confrontation with the simulated marketplace had a significant role in making these executives produce a better product. They had to face the competition head on, hear first-hand – unmediated – consumer response, and as a result they improved not only the advertising of the product but also the product itself.

Pulse research is very expensive. Creating a pulse site requires enormous planning, immense logistical expertise, many, many people, support staff, time, devotion to detail, briefing, analysis, interpretation, money and much more. However, the important lessons of cultural anthropology should not be forgotten in market research. If you want to understand how a culture functions, you must go to the site where it takes place, immerse yourself, watch, listen, speak, observe and participate. Pulse research is a form of research derivative from the lessons of cultural anthropology and we adapted it to resolve our clients' problems.

chapter nineteen

It's Ours
The Petro-Canada Story

The world became traumatized by the 1973 oil crisis. No one expected it. Oil prices rose dramatically. There was a panic about oil supplies and every country was deeply affected. Canada seemed to be quite fortunate in terms of a response because it was, indeed, a producer of significant amounts of oil. However, in 1973 all of Canada's oil production and distribution was foreign-owned.

The Trudeau government was re-elected in 1974 and, unlike in 1972, this time with a majority of parliamentary seats. Trudeau was determined to move boldly on a variety of fronts while he had a majority. The oil crisis was one such front.

In 1975, the government of Canada through an Act of Parliament created a national oil company – Petro-Canada. Although Petro-Canada was an engine of economic growth and development, it was also part of the nation-building strategy of the Trudeau government at the time.

National symbols play an important part in any nation. At the time of the formation of Petro-Canada, there were very few such symbols clearly visible and prominent in all parts of Canada. Whatever symbols existed, such as the Canadian flag, were too remote, too obscure in most people's lives. We had our banks, a protected industry in Canada, in every town and city of the nation. Every town and city and every highway had oil companies and gas stations, but all these oil companies were internationally owned and controlled.

In a very bold and controversial move, the Trudeau government created Petro-Canada. It bought out Fina and Gulf and thus created a distribution system in every town and city and a presence on every highway of the nation.

We were retained by Petro-Canada to develop a strategy that would make it effective. Bill Hopper had already developed Petro-Canada's logo. The maple leaf in the logo declared to all that this was a Canadian company. It gave all Canadians a visual symbol everywhere, in their faces, and gave them a sense of pride in being Canadian, especially when there was recognition that oil supply, the life-blood of North America, was being dominated and controlled outside of the country.

How to convince people to switch their focus and their loyalty from another internationally owned and well-known brand to Petro-Canada? To address this problem we did both quantitative and qualitative studies across the country. We presented our research results in a think-tank conference with Murray Cayley, the marketing research manager of Petro-Canada. Our research suggested people gained a sense of doing something for their country by simply buying gas at Petro-Canada.

Based on our qualitative research, we advocated a simple concept that would become the focus of the marketing effort. It was simple, direct and almost obvious. The concept was "It's Ours!" People could relate to it. It meant something to people. Buying at Petro-Canada, now everywhere and visible in the country, gave people confidence not only in Petro-Canada but in the entire government approach to the oil industry. The oil industry now had a large Canadian presence, visible to everybody. By buying at Petro-Canada, people were doing something for their country, for themselves; they could participate in this nation-building effort. A two-word slogan became an effective marketing tool. It became a force for change. It not only affected consumer behaviour, but it also became a force for Canadian nationalism and Canadian pride. "It's Ours" gave people confidence and underlined Canadian values.

The brand took off and cemented the affinity between the public and the product.

Our subsequent research capitalized on the success of our first findings. We developed the concept "Canada First," which was used in Petro-Canada advertising. No other oil company operating in Canada could use this line. We were able to position Petro-Canada very, very clearly in the public's awareness in a unique, special and distinctive manner.

It was this positioning that created affinity between one company, Petro-Canada, and the Canadian public in spite of the fact that they sold a product no different than that of other oil companies. Product differentiation in the case of Petro-Canada was achieved by moving "beyond the brand" and by creating affinity — a special and unique glue between the public and the product.

We began by understanding Canadian values. We did that by understanding Canadian anxieties about their place in North America and the world in the post-1973 era, a world of insecurity and fear of the future. We found a way to transform that anxiety into a sense of pride by creating a new brand — Petro-Canada. Canadians responded because they wanted to see themselves everywhere, in cities, towns, on every roadway and highway. They felt good about themselves. They connected to a symbol. By taking this insight into the concept "It's Ours" and then "Canada First" we not only made Petro-Canada a very competitive retail oil company, but we also moved "beyond brands" and into the territory we call affinity.

Petro-Canada sustained this affinity in subsequent decades with great success. In 1987, there was a separatist government in Quebec. There was anger in western Canada about the national energy policy. Petro-Canada tried to rekindle this Canadian pride and nationalism by becoming the main sponsor of the 1988 Winter Olympics in Calgary. Even people from the West who had opposed the creation of Petro-Canada proudly associated themselves with this tie-in between the Olympics and Petro-Canada.

Some Canadian values have changed over the past three decades. The lesson is that brands must reconfigure themselves to remain convincing within these changing value systems. They must find new manners of communicating with the public and the consumer; they must find the right stories to tell in their advertising if they want to remain relevant and successful.

Affinity, moving beyond brands, always needs to be recreated as society changes. The art of effective storytelling remains an art that must be reinvented every decade, if not sooner.

Searching to go beyond branding to achieve that elusive magic of affinity always remains a challenge.

chapter twenty

The Toronto Star
The Archaeology of Society - Looking for New Sites

Part 1: Classifieds

All societies have artifacts. Many of these artifacts can be found right under our noses, if we know where to look. Each society creates its own artifacts that reveal some fundamental features of that society. Every society creates its own archaeological sites!

Good market researchers are always on the prowl to locate these sites.

Where do we find the artifacts? Where do we find these archaeological sites?

Newspapers, if we understand them properly, are enormous repositories of artifacts. They must be looked at as sites, as an archaeologist's dream. It's all there historically, and arguably, still important today. Before the advent of the Internet and Craigslist, the richest site of any newspaper was the classified advertisements. It was all in the classified ads.

If anybody wants to mine one of the richest veins of

any society, go to the classifieds. Treat the classifieds as an archaeological site. Gold-digging in classifieds reveals the artifacts of a society.

The classified section of any newspaper has historically been a huge revenue generator. It is estimated that, at their height, 30 per cent of the readership of newspapers went to the classifieds on a daily basis. One may well ask, why would anybody read the classifieds if they were not looking for a job or home, or buying or selling something?

We undertook research for our client, the *Toronto Star*. We tried to understand the power and the role of classifieds. We came to the conclusion that classifieds at that time performed a community function and should be thought of as an archaeological site that exposes, on a daily basis, the goods and services the society requires to function.

Anybody could know the worth or value of their job or their house or their household item. Regardless of their needs, curiosities or interests, they could find them in the classifieds. If they were interested in eroticism, it was there. If they needed part-time labour, if they wanted to sell a used coat – everything that takes place in the community on a daily basis was found in the classifieds. The classifieds make people feel comfortable in the world where they live because it exposed to them almost everything they needed.

People like to participate in their community. The classifieds allowed people to engage, in a vicarious manner, in the transactions of their society. Knowing about buying and selling, knowing what people want and what they need, knowing what value people place on commodities, whatever it may be – labour, cars, products, sex – everything was found in the classifieds. No wonder it was a major part of our engagement with society.

Understanding the role of classifieds allowed the *Star* to develop marketing strategies and pricing strategies to maintain its domination over competitor newspapers. As long as the *Star* dominated in classifieds, it could dominate circulation. Other newspapers, of course, also understand the critical role classifieds play in the competition between newspapers in a market. Competition is always fierce.

By doing a series of group interviews, we were able to understand the central role classifieds played in different segments of society: women, men, older people and younger people.

Print is no longer the only archaeological site to be examined. Craigslist, eBay and other online sites have displaced the once dominant position of print classifieds. Consumer behaviour is changing, driven by new technologies and new means of communication. However, classifieds still play a vital role in people's lives. Searching these archaeological sites, examining the many artifacts of any society and culture through its classified sites – print and also electronic – gives us an understanding as to how that society works, what are its values and preoccupations.

In the 21st century, we can no longer look only to print

or electronic classified ads. The world has changed. The nuggets of our society are now revealed in many other places as well. Social networking is generating many new sites to be examined carefully. And in those new sites, we are discovering a lot of gossip. People are able to express themselves to each other, to find out about each other, to share.

If you go back into history, it is worth asking how and where did people find out about what was going on around them? There was no indoor plumbing, so people, mainly women, went to the well to get their water. And at the well, they found others and shared news, views, conversation. It was there that they found out who needed what, what was changing, who was having a child, who died, and more. The well played the role where both news and gossip was exchanged.

Over the course of centuries, the well evolved into the classifieds. All newspapers had them and still have them. They functioned well for over half a century and performed a very valuable function. Today, the same needs of exchanging news and gossip remain, but the location is shifting into the social networks and blogs of the electronic media.

The human requirement to know has not gone away or vanished. The human requirement for effective story-telling in gossip has not disappeared. Gossip makes us feel comfortable in our own skins. It makes us feel comfortable in our communities. It allows us to share in those communities. When print newspapers played a central role in our societies many sections of the newspaper, including classifieds, performed many of these functions. Today, we must also look to other sites, electronic sites, which appear to be in direct competition with print.

How to influence behaviour? First, you must understand that behaviour. Where are these patterns revealed? You can find them in many hidden places, the many sites of a society, including the classifieds. Look for them. Look for the values because they drive behaviour. Attitudes are many; they change all the time. They may be interesting as curiosa, but they do not reveal the values. Values can be lodged in artifacts. Artifacts are found in sites! The marketplace is abuzz with endless varieties of artifacts, each one open to consideration and analysis.

Part 2: The *Toronto Star* Polls –
Creating Your Own Exclusive News

In the mid-1970s, Martin Goodman was the editor of the *Toronto Star*. He was concerned about product differentiation. He recognized that all the newspapers in his market were covering the same stories at City Hall, at the provincial legislature in Queen's Park, and in Ottawa at the level of national politics. International news seemed to be covered from newspaper to newspaper almost the same way. Everybody relied on the same news sources. The sameness of the media disturbed him.

What could the *Toronto Star* do that would give it exclusive content that no other newspaper or other medium would have? How to breakaway out of the "pack"? How to differentiate the Toronto Star from its competitors?

We were asked to study this problem for Mr. Goodman. We did a series of group interviews with Toronto Star readers. We discovered that they were very interested in subjects that normally were not in newspapers but that could be best covered through polling data.

People were most interested in reading "exclusive" news on a range of subjects, news that would be exclusive to the Toronto Star alone and not found in any other medium or newspaper. The solution to Mr. Goodman's concern for a point of differentiation for the Toronto Star was found.

We recommended that we conduct a survey for the Toronto Star, exclusively, every three months with a large enough sample to be statistically reliable. We would survey the public on 10 or 12 subjects that were of interest to the average Toronto Star reader. We would then report the results as exclusive content to the Toronto Star.

The research directed us to the idea that we would create news and content exclusive to the Toronto Star on topics of interest to its readers on a regular basis and that would give the Toronto Star a product advantage, a point of absolute differentiation. And, of course, the point of product differentiation is, indeed, also the basis of branding.

By creating this series of articles based on exclusive polling for the Toronto Star, the newspaper was able to differentiate itself from all the competition. But equally important was the fact that this exclusive content became a way to encourage advertisers who wanted to be in newspaper sections where news was breaking. The point of differentiation also became a commercial advantage!

Over a period of time, we learned that polling changed how the newspaper functioned. People wanted to hear and to read about themselves through polls. They didn't want filters, such as columnists or commentators, to interpret what was happening in a city, in a country, in an election contest. It made no difference what the subject may be, politics, censorship, health, spending, consumer behaviour or whatever, people wanted to hear and read and learn about themselves. That is what polling does. It allows people to find out whether they themselves are typical or atypical of the general public. They find out all of this by reading the results of polls.

In the 1970s, the efforts by the *Toronto Star* were quite unique. Polling was used in a new way – to make news itself, to influence people and to affect public policy. Today, polling in newspapers and in the media is commonplace.

Part 3: The Conscience of the Community

Story-telling is most effective when it is able to reverberate with the listeners. People will listen to those to whom they feel close, and with whom they can identify.

The *Toronto Star* commissioned us to do a study in order to understand its constituency, to better appreciate the public that it served as a newspaper. The purpose of the study was to understand 10 different ethnic groups in Toronto: how they felt about living in the city, whether they experienced prejudice at work, at home, at school. We wanted to know what they felt were the inhibitions to their opportunities and future.

By commissioning this research, the *Toronto Star* was making a public statement that they were interested in the minority communities of the city. They announced publicly that they wanted to give a voice to immigrants, to minority groups and the results of that voice would be made known widely and clearly! They wanted to tap into and become the public conscience for these new immigrant groups.

The *Toronto Star* published the results of our research.

But they went further. They held a series of public forums whereby the results of the study would be discussed publicly. In addition, they ensured that members of the different Toronto agencies, like the police and the fire department, be present.

These public forums were very well attended and the *Toronto Star* reported on them. The public became engaged with the *Star* in at least two ways: first, by reading about themselves and their problems in print; and second, by attending these public forums and then reading about their own discussions or confrontations with public agencies in the city. The *Toronto Star* positioned itself, therefore, as the brave and public conscience of its readership and, by extension, of the city. The results were significant. The *Toronto Star* used polling to create news, but, also by discussing the results of these polls in public forums, they began to affect public policy at the local level.

The *Toronto Star* started off with a marketing problem. But the research we generated became a force for change. That is what marketing can do. It can be used as a force for significant change. From the *Star*'s perspective, it was their exclusive content based on our polling that created an ethos in the city specific to the *Star* that no other newspaper could achieve. For instance, their commissioned research exposed that people felt discriminated against, not only because they were not able to be employed by organizations like the police but some groups (blacks, Asians and others) felt that the police targeted them unjustly. People felt that the police were prejudiced in their behaviour.

The *Toronto Star*, of course, was a business. But by using polling, reporting on that polling in an exclusive manner, creating public forums and reporting on those, the *Star*, indeed, became the moral conscience of the Toronto community. The feelings of the community, or a major part of the community, were not reported as hearsay, but were substantiated by polling results. The polling confirmed perceptions and the public debate about those results affected public policy. And this resulted in increased affinity for the *Star* by Torontonians – especially those in communities who felt they were given a voice for the first time – that still exists today. The *Star* both affected public policy and strengthened its business with this new strategy.

chapter twenty-one

Choice Marketing
Empowering the Consumer in Different Cultures

— — — — — — — — — — —

In any culture, there are moments where consumers make purchasing decisions. Our challenge is to find those moments, or opportunities and to decipher the ways consumer choices and decisions are made.

For example, market research has shown us that people have learned to wait for sales. The consumer in the marketplace has been educated to wait. Most people are not that anxious to be first in the line for a product. However, there are exceptions; for example, the iPod where many people waited in line to be first. But when it comes to fashion, more and more people are waiting for sales. The same with electronics, TV sets and endless other consumer items. The psyche has adjusted to wait, especially for the savvy consumer, especially for big ticket items, like cars. You wait for the sale knowing the "day will come."

Consumers recognize products as they relate to their own culture. Cultures are ways of life. Cultures reflect values and values are guiding principles for behaviour. And consumers can be heavily influenced by the sense that they are getting value for their money. If a product is positioned within a consumers' own culture, they retain positive affection for it. It is something they recognize as having a relationship with them. Consumers act in their own self-interest. If they can get better value for their hard-earned money, they will make those choices that enhance the value for money.

Ford was a minor player in the car industry in Europe for many years (except for the UK where they not only had a significant market share but also had become the largest selling brand). In the 1980s the challenge was to find a way to move European consumers to Ford. Ford was not a European brand. Ford had brand recognition because it was a global product, but it lacked a national pedigree in Europe. Peugeot was French, Fiat was Italian, and Volkswagen was German. The challenge was to find a way to create a market opportunity for Ford within European countries that would have an impact.

The question, obviously, was how. Should one approach all countries in Europe in the same manner? Where to start, with what marketing strategy, in what manner?

In developing any marketing strategy, it is always important to ask, Is there a big idea, a big concept that can address the problem? At the same time, one must remember that all consumer experience takes place within a specific culture; if effective advertising is story-telling, it must be recognized within a given culture.

The solution to Ford's problem in Europe was to provide the consumers in different countries with value propositions that would convince them to move to Ford. In our research we recognized an opportunity that did not change the product. It wasn't a technical breakthrough that would be the lever for change in consumer behaviour. However, we found a concept, an idea, that proved to be successful, first in Italy and then in other countries. There are two chapters to this story.

The Italian Strategy

The first takes place in Italy, where Ford experimented with innovative marketing ideas. In the mid- to late-1980s, the head of Ford Italy was Massimo Ghenzer. Ghenzer had a profound understanding of Italian culture. He innately understood the values that would influence Italian purchasing decisions – family, safety, love of children and value for money.

Ford was also up against Fiat. In the 1970s and into the 1980s, most Italians were still buying their first vehicles. Entry-level cars were utilitarian vehicles; they had a function, but they were not thought to be luxury items. Of course, there were luxury vehicles in the marketplace, but the strategy of Ford was to go after the entry-level vehicle market.

In a brilliant stroke of marketing ingenuity, Ghenzer introduced air conditioning in its entry-level vehicle, the Ford Fiesta. He effectively told the Italian consumer that with a Ford vehicle, they could experience air conditioning. They could experience luxury in a low-end vehicle at competitive prices.

Marketing creates a point of differentiation in the marketplace for your product. Doing so creates awareness and awareness is a step towards influencing purchasing decisions. Ghenzer called it the end of the "utilitarian" era. He positioned Ford as the company with leading-edge thinking for average Italian families.

Under Ghenzer, Ford was the first company in Italy to introduce airbags in an entry-level vehicle, again, the Fiesta. The advertising proclaimed Ford Fiesta was "beauty with conscience." It encouraged people to become conscious of safety and Ford was leading the way with its airbags in every Fiesta. In an even bolder move, at the world famous Italian music festival in San Remo, Ghenzer told the story to the Italian public on TV: "If you are going to buy a car, even if it is not a Ford, buy one with an airbag." No other car in Italy had airbags as standard equipment, not Fiat, not Volkswagen. Ghenzer did not tell Italians to buy Ford. Rather he highlighted for them one of the intrinsic Italian values – children, safety, family, security. Values drive human behaviour. The conclusion obviously was that if you value those Italian values, you would be driven to buy the car with airbags, the Ford product. Making airbags standard equipment gave Ford a point of differentiation where values centred on children, family and value for money.

The move was further extended with another brilliant advertising campaign centred on the values of children, family and value for money. Story-telling incorporated these values in Ford's Christmas advertising. It was Christmas, a time for family, a time when the values of a culture, especially Italian culture, are brought forward and become very salient. In its Christmas advertising, Ford showed a beautiful face of a baby and admonished people to buy a car with an airbag.

With these bold moves, over a period of a couple of years, Ford had created a public awareness in Italy and an association in their minds for safety and airbags. It further proclaimed that every car purchaser, regardless of what kind of vehicle they bought, luxury or entry-level, should be fully conscious of the need for safety, for themselves, their children and their families.

The advertising tapped into the value system of the Italian public. It affected the consciousness of the consumer and it positioned Ford on the side of the average consumer. Of course, what Ford had done was buy up all the capacity in Europe for airbag production so that, effectively, the competition could not respond to this market challenge quickly.

The next move in the Italian marketplace was also very bold. It was the introduction of choice marketing. How did it work?

To further differentiate Ford from its competition, it

said to the consumer, if you come to Ford, you can buy any vehicle – they are all at the same price. You can choose between a three-door, four-door or five-door vehicle. You make the choice. You decide. No penalty, no premium, all at the same price. The five-door vehicle was obviously more expensive, but Ford said to the consumer, buy whatever suits you and get the best value for your money.

Most people with families, of course, chose the five-door, the wagon. People recognized the value proposition and Ford's willingness to empower the consumer with the choice without extra cost.

Everybody talked about it. The press talked about it. Ford soon became the number one seller of wagons in Italy. Anybody in the market for a wagon had to consider Ford. From a marketing perspective, Ford had become a serious player in the marketplace. It had more than doubled its share, to 10 per cent!

Choice marketing was further extended to the engine. The consumer could choose between a petrol and diesel engine – at the same price. Diesels cost more to manufacture than petrol, but the strategy of choice marketing further consolidated Ford as a serious player in the Italian market. Ford sold more diesels because it was better value for money, even though the Ford diesel was somewhat inferior to the competitions' products.

The genius of this choice marketing strategy was that incentive was not price-driven. It did not get Ford into a price war with the competition. It did not cut prices. Rather, the genius was that it was product opportunity driven. It trusted the consumer. Ford was successful in Italy because it recognized the values of the Italian consumer, the values of Italian culture and the Italian family. It empowered the Italian consumer to look towards Ford – you get more value for your money, you make the choices. Ford was on the right side and on the consumers' side.

By adopting this marketing strategy, Ford became a serious player in a market where it had been a very small player. It became a leader, it gave it a point of view and it won respect and a position in the marketplace. People were attracted to Ford because they knew that if they wanted value for their money, they had to look towards Ford!

If this Ford strategy worked in Italy for Ford, could it work in other European countries?

The German Strategy

In the 1980s Germany had developed a program to stimulate automobile sales called Clean Air & Safety. It offered a cash incentive of 2000 DMs to encourage trade-ins of old and dirty vehicles. The cars had to be 10 years old to qualify for the cash rebate. The program applied to all vehicles sold in Germany. A new car was now more affordable. The opportunity was there.

Duncan Rooke was the marketing executive at Ford Germany at the time. He looked at the success of Ford in

Italy and he decided to introduce the same program in Germany. In conjunction, these two programs, one offered by the government, the other by Ford, allowed Ford to progress in Germany.

Successful advertising is about telling stories that reverberate and connect the viewer or listener to the story told. Ford decided to focus on the most German of all German artifacts, something which was known and recognizable to everybody and one that connected people to the artifact.

In Germany, Ford was the Escort. How to get Germans to look seriously at and buy the Escort? It was not a Volkswagen, not a German car. The answer lay in associating the Ford Escort with German artifacts, with German culture.

What is more German than the Rhine River and a Rhine River barge? We had the artifact. Now we had to associate this artifact with the Ford Escort. Ford went to the Rhine River and found a Rhine River barge. They mounted a Ford Escort on the back of the Rhine River barge. Effectively, they showed that Ford was, indeed, part of a very, very German way of living. Ford understood the heart and soul of Germany. These barges were perfect German images and they reflected a way of life, the independent German entrepreneur. By hitching itself to this very German artifact, the Ford Escort identified itself with German values. It had become German.

Ford management also brought to Germany the one-price or choice-marketing strategy that had worked so well in Italy. Now, the German consumers could make their own choice: a three-, four- or five-door vehicle at no extra cost and no penalty to the consumer. Ford empowered the German consumer, not Volkswagen, not BMW. Ford trusted them to decide for themselves whatever was in their best interest. They would decide the best value for their money.

The program in Germany, as in Italy, proved to be a great success. Ford sold a lot of wagons. Ford wagons were everywhere in Germany. Ford ultimately achieved an 11 per cent share in Germany.

Germans for the most part buy German products. Roughly two-thirds of German cars sold are German-manufactured. Buying a German car is easy. It is the norm. Buying a brand that is not German is a statement and not easy to do for most people in Germany. It is a statement that says that German is not good enough! Ford had to find a way to succeed in this difficult environment.

Value is always an incentive to purchase in almost any culture. Germans, like the Italians, recognized the value and the choice-marketing opportunity that Ford presented. Ford succeeded in this very competitive German market because it had a point of view based on this strategy. The point of view inspired people to buy Ford wagons. Anybody interested in a wagon had to consider the value of the Ford proposition. It positioned Ford very successfully in the market.

The same strategy was soon applied in England and then in Canada and then in Brazil. The objective was to associate

Ford with a value proposition that would attract consumers. But, at the same time, the objective was not to start a price war – no discounts, no rebates. Just more value for your money and in any culture it was clear that people would behave in their own self-interest. People bought wagons because they understood value. Ford became the dominant seller of wagons. By transferring this choice to the consumer, a trust was established between the consumer and the brand. Consumer values (as demonstrated by the value of value for money) seemed to be the same everywhere: Europe, North America, England and Brazil.

chapter twenty-two

Price-Point-Package Marketing

Over many years of study, it is obvious to us that consumers like transparency.

Choice is complicated in the marketplace. It can be confusing. It may create stress and anxiety. Choice, especially with very expensive consumer items such as homes and cars, may actually provoke fear. In our research with car purchasers, we know that some consumers are afraid of going to a car dealership because they want to avoid an encounter with a salesperson. They even visit car lots when the dealership or the lot is not open to avoid this encounter.

In relation to Ford, we discovered that although people had an interest in Ford vehicles, some potential purchasers had a visceral dislike, or they anticipated a dislike for the purchasing experience.

Some people could not understand the pricing structure. Others were confused by the many options offered to them. The "extras" could be very costly. There were too many choices to be made.

How to resolve these walls to purchasing a vehicle? Was there a way to renew the positive side of purchasing a vehicle? Was it possible to make the purchasing experience a positive experience?

The solution was "price-point-package marketing." It was quite simple. Basically, you bundled a variety of options into one single package. For example, you would place power windows, enhanced carpeting, tinted windows and other options in one package. Instead of adding all of these options separately into the base price of the car, you bundled the options and set one price for the package. The consumer would be presented with the details of the package and they would say yes or no.

By bundling the options, it was obvious to the consumer that they were getting very good value for their money because the package was significantly cheaper than purchasing every item in the option package separately. As well, to make the purchasing experience even more positive, the price was clearly visible to the consumer. Every vehicle would have the price, including the option package, fixed on the rear window. It was printed in black and white and visible so that everybody could see.

Placing the price clearly and honestly on each car in the lot so that everybody could see it transformed the purchasing experience for many people. Much of the fear, anxiety, almost loathing, that people had expressed dissipated. The result of price-point-package marketing was that Ford made money, the consumer got better value for their money, and there was more transparency in the purchasing transaction.

Consumers want a positive experience in the market-place. Shopping is not just about buying a product; it is also now an experience, an almost aesthetic experience. We have created physical spaces to enhance the consumer experience. We have malls, shopping centres and gallerias. We have created architecture and shopping spaces with a view to enhance the purchasing experience.

Buying a car is a very intense and expensive purchasing moment for a consumer in our society. The strategy of price-point-package marketing alleviated many negative feelings and experiences in the process. It assured the consumer better value for their money. Ford was an innovator in marketing and this strategy proved to be successful to the consumer and profitable for the company.

chapter twenty-three

Consumer Values
The Need for Newness – A Ford Success Story
━ ━

Most people buy cars on payments. The North American industry is built on this. People buy cars and pay for them in four to five years. Leased cars, traditionally, are a four-year deal.

In the research we conducted for Ford in the 1980s, we learned that after owning a Ford for two years, most people were quite satisfied with the product and the experience. In fact, many of them indicated after two years that they loved their vehicle. The problems arose after that initial two-year period. The research showed that during the next three years of ownership, customer satisfaction decreased significantly.

The industry research also showed that by comparison, Honda and Toyota owners' satisfaction increased from year 1 to year 5. At the end of the five-year cycle, Honda and Toyota owners were more satisfied with the performance of their vehicles. The evidence from the research was clear and it posed a significant challenge for Ford.

The basic question challenging the company and the

marketing issue was simple – how to get people out of their Ford vehicles after two years when they were quite happy and avoid the decline in satisfaction that increased significantly beyond those first two years of ownership?

The concept and the solution were quite simple. We came up with the "two-year lease" concept. Put people into Ford vehicles on a two-year-lease arrangement and the consumer would make low payments during that period of the lease. Americans love cars and they love new cars!

The benefits to the consumer were huge. A two-year lease meant that monthly payments were lower than if they had locked themselves into a four-year-lease arrangement. It tapped into the American desire to buy new cars. Newness is good to most consumers! They could love their new cars more often than ever before. In theory at least, they could get into a new car every two years on a lease arrangement. The solution was consistent with the American consumer's value system. The solution not only put people into cars more often but also created an entirely new ownership segment in the population.

We tested two-year leasing very carefully. The issue was how to explain a new way of experiencing a new vehicle every two years so that people could understand the benefit. The communication had to tap into people's desires and values – stability, trouble-free, desire for newness, low monthly payments and sense of privilege. And the bragging rights of showing the neighbour a new car every two years.

Nothing actually changed. The product did not change. The vehicles were not improved. The solution lay in understanding the issue of payments and in tapping into the value system of car purchasing. The qualitative research indicated a solution to a problem that did, however, radically change the buying cycle: instead of buying a car every four years, people traded in their vehicles every two years.

As long as residual values could support the two-year cycle, this proved to be a brilliant strategy that consumers loved and it made Ford a lot of money. This same two-year-lease program was introduced in other parts of the world and proved to be quite successful in Canada and Britain.

This is an example of understanding the desire for newness in terms of the values of a population. The two-year-lease program clearly understood the values and dreams of the American consumer and, at the same time, this marketing strategy was a force for change in the entire automotive industry. The solution worked because it tapped into consumer values. It capitalized on the experience the consumer had with new cars from Ford, at least for the first two years…a new car, a warranty, no problems, and, the prospect of another new vehicle in two years!

The solution reinforced a fundamental value in the American experience. People like to drive and to have access to new cars, new models. The solution ensured that the American was not tied to his car for a long time. If they disliked it, in two years' time, they had another one. By doing the research, by understanding that the solution to the Ford problem lay in the value system of the American public, we could affect and alter the buying cycle and the behaviour of the consumer.

One of the very important consequences of this marketing strategy developed at Ford was that the buying cycle of the American car buyer changed. Instead of "newness" being defined in a four-to-five-year cycle, the buying cycle was now two years. Ford effectively guaranteed the consumer a residual value on any new car they sold at 50 per cent of the original selling price. By doing so, the entire industry was changed. Many people wanted to and got into new cars every two years.

By changing the purchase pattern, consumers were happy. Ford was happy because they were selling more new cars with more equipment. The company made money. But the risks were very high because they had to guarantee the residual value after two years. They soon realized that they could not always meet that guarantee. They started to lose money. They had to change the lease program!

This is a classic example of marketing as a force for change. The program changed the way people lived and the way they bought cars. It recognized the values of the desire for newness and of cars with more features that would increase satisfaction. By understanding the underlying principles of behaviour, namely, values, Ford was able to change purchasing behaviour through an effective marketing strategy.

chapter twenty-four

Let Us Compare Cultures
Ford vs. Toyota

Over many years, we worked for many companies and conducted hundreds of studies in numerous countries and many cultures. We worked extensively in the auto industry for Ford and later, for Toyota. It is instructive to reflect on our experiences with these two major global companies.

Ford ran as an American company everywhere, no matter in which country or in which culture they were located. They brought with them their own corporate culture that reflected American values. While they always had a deep sensitivity to the country in which they located themselves, and recognized that both marketing and product development had to reflect that country, Ford never abandoned the values that drove their own corporate culture.

Ford treated their women employees everywhere as if they were working in the United States. They demanded, everywhere, respect for women, fewer restrictions on women and expected a commitment to the American work ethic everywhere.

Ford companies in Mexico or Spain always worked on

time. The Ford work ethic, consistent with the American work ethic, prevailed. Ford executives in Spain, Mexico, or France arrived very early and worked until very late, much like they did in Detroit. Their approach to business practices everywhere, especially in terms of their highly prized financial accounting system, were enforced everywhere. In terms of corporate culture, US values and the US work ethic prevailed everywhere Ford went.

Toyota ran everywhere as a Japanese company or at least recognized their Japanese roots. In Europe, where we worked with Toyota, they worked as a European company with a distinctive overlay of Japanese values. Although there were European CEOs at the executive level, the CEO's office always had a Japanese "shadow" who was directly responsible to and reported to the Japanese head office. In other less significant areas, the corporate culture maintained a Japanese touch, such as always having Japanese-style food available in the company cafeteria. They used Japanese terms in their daily conversations, such as *kaizen* and *genchi genbutsu*. The "J" factor became very much part of working for Toyota.

Each global car manufacturer was firmly rooted in its home country; in terms of the culture of these two great companies, the result was enormous differences that reflected different value systems and approaches to the marketplace. These differences deeply affected their product, their production, their value systems, their understanding of the consumer, their marketing and, of course, their vehicles.

At Toyota, quality is king and the chief engineer is king. Engineering defines quality and quality is enshrined in the corporate culture. Toyota, as a global company, manufactures their vehicles in some 140 different plants in different countries. Their objective is to ensure that quality production obliterates the question of where their vehicles are made. The brand, regardless of place of manufacture, assures the uniformity of quality. In new product development, the chief engineer at Toyota made choices driven by quality concerns. Design would be compromised for quality.

Not so at Ford. When we did research for Ford in North America, we had occasion to compare door panels between a Camry and Taurus. We discovered that in the Camry there were two pieces, in the Taurus many pieces. Two welds were in Camry rear-light assembly, numerous welds in a Taurus. Which rear-light assembly was more likely to leak over time? The Taurus door looked better. The Camry lasted longer.

Toyota built their reputation on the centrality of the concept of quality. And the consumer learned that and liked it. They read *Consumer Reports* and other quality reports on Toyota. The results were consistent over many years. The consumer, slowly but surely, absorbed the lesson from Toyota.

Quality was always the mission of Toyota. The success of Toyota in the North American market took a few decades. The consumer learned that Toyota meant quality. And quality triumphed over the Big Three in America.

In today's marketplace the point of differentiation is

neither environment sensitivity nor safety. Today sensitivity about the environment is a given. Everybody knows it and does it. Environmental sensitivity and safety are both givens. Everybody knows them and must abide by them. To defy these givens in the new marketplace is to assure irrelevance. Quality, however, is a point of differentiation. It may take some time before the consumer recognizes it in a brand, or a product line. But quality is a hallmark of a product, built up slowly over time and tested constantly by the savvy, informed consumer.

Contrast Toyota to Ford.

At Ford, the designer was king. Ford depended on marketing and used design as the impulse motivator. The Ford philosophy was about first impressions. They believed that the impulse to beauty and attractiveness drives consumer choice. You sell product and provoke consumer choice by design. Marketing draws people's attention to design. The culture of Toyota makes marketing a secondary activity. To Toyota, the consumer is a rational person and will choose quality over everything else.

Ford emphasized design, impressions, colours and shapes in their product strategy over technology and quality. They used insights about consumers, such as our research on touch zones, to create derivatives of old products to put into the marketplace in order to succeed. They believed that the aesthetics of design could camouflage quality defectives underneath.

Toyota used engineering quality to develop and sustain

quality, assuming that consumer choice in the long term would be rational rather than impulsive.

The differences between Ford and Toyota used to be impulse versus reason, design versus quality. Toyota had a deep faith in quality execution while Ford put its faith in design and exterior nuances.

This was a very instructive and powerful tale of two corporate cultures. The verdict came in. Ultimately, you win in the marketplace on a long-term commitment to quality rather than on impulsive, short-term emotional choices.

In recent years, Ford has learned the lesson. They "retooled" themselves and improved their concerns with quality. Today, their products are sold not just for design, the look, but also for quality. The renewed success of Ford now is driven by quality. They never forget to tell the consumer in their marketing and advertising that they are very confident about quality. They also remind the consumer that they are sensitive to the environment, their cars get good mileage and also, of course, their vehicles look good!

There is always a difficult balance to be achieved between the need for quality and the consumer appetite for novelty. The story of Toyota in Europe is intriguing. Toyota was gaining market share; they wanted a 5 per cent share by 2008. The press and the public had come to respect Toyota products. Even VW acknowledged this. The head of VW was said to have commented, "If they ever learned how to market, watch out!"

Then, Toyota introduced the new Aurus into Europe. The

market research showed it had deficiencies. Consumers were cool on the product, not hot. Initial sales looked okay, but the car did not take off. People had expectations about Toyota, but these expectations did not pan out. The product was a letdown. The promise was there, but the quality was a disappointment. Toyota created expectations that disappointed. The new product did not satisfy the expectations. Features were deficient; plastic was perceived to be cheap. The product was deficient not only in its looks but also in features that the public had come to expect from Toyota. The public punished the producer.

In retrospect, one can view this experience in Europe as a precursor of what has happened in North America and worldwide today. It was a prelude to the Toyota misfortune today, as it is being played out globally. When Toyota's difficulties emerged in North America, senior management's first instinct was to assert that the problems in fact did not exist; they said the problems were in people's imagination. They shirked responsibility and tried to bully consumers into thinking they were responsible and the product was infallible. By doing so, Toyota signalled they were no longer the company people thought they were: profits came first and customer satisfaction was secondary. Finally, Toyota had to admit their fallibility and they have been publicly humbled not only in North America but also worldwide, even in Japan. The corporate invincibility of Toyota has collapsed!

The real issue is that there was a change of values in

Toyota where customer satisfaction through quality had previously been sacrosanct. It first appeared that Toyota had caught the American disease of not listening to the customer. That is what got the American industry in trouble. They thought they could get away with it. Poor quality cannot be hidden or camouflaged. The rapid pace whereby Toyota fell from grace is most instructive. It plays into the enormous changes that are taking place among consumers, consumer culture and the marketplace.

The introduction of the Aurus was the first time that Toyota took shortcuts at the cost of consumer satisfaction. It was the first time that senior management took a decision knowing that they would disappoint consumers. But they went ahead willingly!

The "new" Toyota, deeply damaged and very humbled, is playing out high corporate drama, globally. This is an important lesson to global companies since it signals the emergence of a more robust and empowered global consumer culture.

There is a public wisdom in the marketplace. People in the marketplace make choices in their own self-interest. They cannot be fooled all the time. Their experiences with products are, indeed, authentic. They can be very loyal. They can become attached to a brand. As we are now learning, the new global consumer can be very persistent, can build allies globally and can successfully take on and humble global corporate giants.

The collective consensus is the genius of the market-place. People make decisions in their own self-interest. Word of mouth is the great elixir but it is also the great destroyer. And, today, nothing can be kept a secret for very long!

Affinity takes a long time to develop. Part of affinity is the consistent delivery, over time, on a promise of the brand. If that covenant between the brand and the public is eroded or betrayed, affinity dissipates and the brand suffers.

chapter twenty-five

Trenitalia
An Italian Story

Massimo Ghenzer, who had worked at Ford Europe, was appointed head of marketing at Trenitalia, the Italian passenger railway company. He invited me to help him as he set about reorganizing the marketing efforts of the company and turning it around.

Trenitalia was a government-owned and -operated company. As with most companies, they became stuck in their own corporate culture; reflecting the traditional values that had been embedded in the company over decades. In addition, Trenitalia had no marketing urge or instinct to speak of. Many people in the operations leadership of Trenitalia looked at marketing as a waste of time. We were called in to assess the situation and also to make recommendations as to how to inject some new marketing strategies into the company to increase train travel.

I set about trying to understand the values that drove the staff. There was office staff and the ticket-selling staff in the major centres of Rome, Milan and Naples, as well as the drivers, guards and on-train support staff. We interviewed them and tried to listen to them as they explained what they did, why they did what they did, how they understood their own behaviour. In trying to understand how they explained their own behaviour, we began to understand the values that propelled their behaviour.

Fairly quickly, as the staff explained their behaviour, we learned that they hated their uniforms. These uniforms were heavy and cumbersome, especially in hot weather, and throughout Italy and especially in the south, temperatures during the summer can be extremely hot. In addition, the staff thought their uniforms were ugly, poorly made and out of sync with the stylish character of Italian design and clothing.

It was not surprising that given their explanation of these uniforms, most of the Trenitalia staff did not wear them. Ticket-sellers in the train stations all dressed differently and some of them smoked while they sold their tickets. Their disregard for the uniforms extended to their feelings towards the company. The chaotic nature of the staff and their clothing was also reflected in the appearance of the trains. Many of them were covered in graffiti. The trains were filthy both outside and inside. Washrooms were very dirty and many did not function. The stations were littered with paper and trash; the tracks were littered with cigarette butts, plastic bags, debris and other filth. There was a deep sense and appearance of chaos everywhere. Nobody seemed to care, certainly not the staff and, by extension, the executives.

Clearly, the first things to do were to get rid of the graffiti, clean up the trains and stations and, significantly, begin to change the attitudes of the staff. The objective was to restore some sense of pride in the employees and, by extension, to begin to change the look of the trains.

The uniforms had to change. New, more sensible and fashionable uniforms were designed and given to the staff. They began to look better and feel better about themselves. Looking good and feeling better made them take pride in their jobs and Trenitalia. This restoration of pride was extended to the trains themselves. The trains were cleaned up, washrooms were made functional and new standards of cleanliness were established and enforced. When the trains were in the stations, higher standards of cleanliness were maintained. To create a better relationship with the public, self-ticketing was established in many train stations so that the train riders could avoid lineups and have a more immediate link to the new, efficient Trenitalia.

The staff began to feel that the leadership of the company cared about them and they reciprocated by caring about their jobs, how they looked and their relationship to the public. Respect between the staff and the consumer was established.

The second part of the restructuring was to establish three core brands for Trenitalia and to find a way to market them effectively. The three brands were: the Eurostar, the night train and the commuter train. Mr. Ghenzer established three brand managers and gave each of them a clear mission to create an identity. And with that identity, he asked them to establish a marketplace for each of the brands. For each brand we created a brand bull's eye with the promise, the values and attributes for each brand. The bull's eyes acted as the core source of thinking for the brand managers.

Changing a corporate culture is not just creating some ads and marketing. It also involves retraining the executive-level staff. Mr. Genzer established a training program that was equivalent to an MBA course with a focus on the principles of marketing. I taught this intensive two-day training program to 40 people every three months; for a year and a half, a new group was trained each quarter.

With brand managers, with an executive training program, with a focus on marketing, the objective was to create a feeling that Trenitalia wanted to create an elite marketing community in Italy. These very high objectives were received positively by staff and the executives.

However, there was more to do. When Italy changed from the lire to the euro as the standard of currency, there was confusion among the public, in Italy and elsewhere. Not only were we trying to change Trenitalia itself, but we also had to cope with a public that was now alienated from many consumer activities because of the change in currency.

We came up with an idea that would deal with both problems.

Our idea was to offer a special one-price train ticket, valid only on Saturday, but valid for train travel between any two train stops, or cities anywhere in Italy. The price would be something simple, something that was recognizable. It was to be 10 euros. Everybody could understand 10 euros. Compared with the old lire, 10 seemed like a small number. We effectively introduced the new currency through a new product and pricing structure on the train company.

The Saturday product became a subbrand of Trenitalia: Trenitalia Sabato. It was an enormous success. On the first Saturday, one hundred and forty-two thousand more people travelled on the train than any previous Saturday. Many of these Saturday train travellers had never taken a train before. They were able to travel to many places in Italy where they had never been before. They went to see family and friends. They went to explore their own country. The train was a vehicle of transportation and also of fun. Trenitalia was not just a marketer of train seats on a rebranded and cleaned-up system, but it became a source of pride and nationalism. Passengers could now do it at an affordable and recognizable price – one single price.

Trenitalia Sabato was more than a price for a ticket. It was an innovative way to travel but also it succeeded in rebranding the entire company. People took pride in their trains, whereas previously they told jokes and laughed at the "old" service. It became an organization that actually engendered pride in the public and in the staff. The staff was galvanized, imbued with a new culture and a new set of values. Their behaviour changed. They were excited. Trenitalia was doing something for the average Italian citizen that nobody else had done. As a government-owned system, Trenitalia was delivering an affordable, excellent service to everybody!

Our research showed that one-half of the Trenitalia Sabato travellers were first-time train users. A new public for train travel was discovered. At 10 euros per ticket, Trenitalia broke even. It later moved to a 12-euro ticket price and it made money at that price.

When we were asked to undertake some research work for Trenitalia, we did not know the Italian train system. We did not consider ourselves expert in train travel nor in Italy. What we tried to do was to approach a real problem by understanding the values that drive human behaviour. In this case it was in the context of Italy and in the context of train travel. By listening to the train staff, we were able to appreciate the values that drove their behaviour. By listening to the public, we began to understand the values that were the guiding principles of their behaviour.

Marketing is a force for change. Our research allowed us to make recommendations to our client and the result allowed them to develop a new and appropriate marketing strategy with new tools and new approaches.

We recognized the values that drove Italian behaviour: frugality because people wanted value for their money;

clarity and simplicity with regard to the new currency of the euro; affection for family and friends and their desire to visit with them; and nationalism, a desire to take pride in their country and things Italian.

The transformed Trenitalia instituted by Mr. Ghenzer was a force for change consistent with the values held dear by Italians. That is why it succeeded.

chapter twenty-six

Turning the Consumer "On"
The Powers of Suggestion
Three Products, Three Stories

Story 1: Hellmann's Mayonnaise

Fairly early in our research experience, I was called by the advertising agency for Hellmann's Mayonnaise. Although this product was well established in the marketplace, sales were stagnant. I was asked to do some research and also to consult on the advertising campaign. I conducted a series of group interviews with consumers, some personal in-depth interviews with chefs, and spent time observing chefs in their kitchens.

My solution was to treat mayonnaise as a sensuous product. By the power of suggestion in the advertising, we created a different personality for this product. The advertising showed mayonnaise being thrown, literally, into salads, almost in an uncontrollable manner. The product was shown as floating, sensuous.

By redefining the sense of the product, by associating

it with sensuality, by associating the product with a sense of joy, almost with sexual characteristics, an aphrodisiac, the consumer saw mayonnaise in a new light. It was no longer a fat product to be wary of, but a product of joy, fun, sensuality, something that enhanced you and your appetite, stimulated and invigorated you. The eating experience laced with mayonnaise was transformed.

Products can assume personalities in the marketplace. In advertising you can portray a product as having a different personality. By the power of suggestion, you can redefine a staid, old product. The research helped define the existing personality of the product. The solution to the marketing problem was to transform the personality of the product. Advertising convinced the consumer of that new and joyful personality.

Story 2: Cadbury's Chocolate

Dave McMillan had retained us when he was at Dad's Cookies. He then sold his company and went to Cadbury's. He called us and retained us to help.

One of the products at Cadbury's was their Caramilk chocolate bar. It was successful, but not growing in the marketplace. We were asked to consult. Could we suggest a new and different marketing approach?

I convinced McMillan to do a study not on Caramilk, but on candy. I wanted to go back to history and study the evolution of candy, to ask, what was the first candy? I wanted to understand the larger picture, the relationship of people to candy. My view was that to understand human behaviour with regard to Caramilk, I had to understand the basic values that drive our consumer response to candy.

My hypothesis was that candy satisfies emotional needs. I thought that a biblical understanding of the role of candy would be an interesting place to begin. I remembered the biblical references to milk and honey. I thought I would begin by interviewing biblical scholars.

One of the most critical interviews I did was with an esteemed thinker and religious leader, a great biblical scholar, Rabbi Gunther Plaut. Why? We were searching for some basic understandings, some historical idea or ideas that would allow us to understand the bigger picture, the historical origins of milk and honey. Often, going to original sources for ideas kindles basic insights that may have profound implications. Rabbi Plaut explained to us that the biblical and historical association with candy was not just "milk and honey" but also there was a second, equally important association, "sex and bread." Both were absolutely necessary for survival. The words for bread and sex had the same root, I was told. In that sense they intellectually shared the same territory. Fundamentally, both associations had the same biblical and historical derivatives. But the idea, clearly, was bigger than we thought when we set out.

We now had the insight, the idea, a better way to understand the relationship of the consumer to candy, and specifically, to Caramilk.

The centre of this candy/chocolate bar was caramel. Caramel was soft, oozing, sensuous; it oozed when released from its chocolate encasement. The association, when presented in advertising, was obvious. The key to transforming the personality of the product and presenting it to the consumer as attractive, suggestive, sensuous and sexual was achieved in the advertising.

Advertising is about tapping into an existing cultural ethos. It is a way of communicating to a public. It is the poetry of the time. It works by images, metaphors, similes, suggestion. By understanding the historical derivatives of milk, honey, caramel, and portraying them to the consumer in a contemporary manner with the right images and sensuality, the product forged a new personality that appealed to the public.

Story 3: Butter

Over a number of years, Goldfarb Consultants was retained by the Dairy Bureau of Canada to do many studies. The Dairy Bureau was always concerned with butter. At the consumer level, butter as a category was struggling.

By the 1980s, the research we conducted for our clients showed that fat was becoming a pariah in society. Medical science had produced a series of studies, widely distributed and discussed, that demonstrated that fat was not very good for you. The producers' interests were in direct conflict with the consumers' interests and were colliding with the new values of the general population. In the marketplace, it was clear that consumer interest would win. The producers would lose.

We then turned our attention to the challenge as to how to sell butter when butter was, clearly, a product with a high-fat content and relatively low nutritional value. However, the up side was that butter had an exceptionally good taste. Our challenge, then, was to find a way of turning the concept of "taste" into a benefit that was different than simple taste. How to enhance the public appreciation and also the perception of taste? In this matrix of perception, how could we change human behaviour to benefit our client and to reposition butter in the marketplace? That is always the marketing question – using marketing as a force for change.

In the tremendously successful film *Tom Jones*, there was an eating scene that was long, engaging and attention-getting. Everybody knew about it and everybody loved it! The scene worked because it was so overly sensuous and sexual. It titillated every viewer. We thought we found the big idea – food as a sensual experience. Do it, eat it, you'll love it! The challenge became clear – how to turn butter, fast becoming a pariah food, into a sensuous food?

We made our recommendations to our client and to the

advertising agency. The idea was to create a series of ani-
mated characters dancing in a very sensuous romantic
manner. These characters represented butter. The music was
very sexy and the characters were all teasing each other in
a very exciting fashion. The message was obvious – butter
was a sensual product, an elixir!

We tested the campaign and found that it created a great
deal of excitement. But, clearly, this would be a controversial campaign for the Dairy Bureau.

In all research, relationships between the researcher and
the client are absolutely crucial. I had developed a close and
trusting relationship with the Dairy Bureau and we were
able to convince them that this campaign should be run.
They did so. The campaign ran for a number of years and
was quite successful. It raised butter consumption, gave
butter a different personality and changed the way people
thought of butter.

The product did not change. Butter remained what it was.
But marketing encouraged people to try it, to use it. There
was much more to butter and the experience of eating butter
than just taste. There was also fun, enjoyment, excitement.

We learned that to get a campaign that is edgy, risky and
that tries to change how a traditional product is perceived
requires management support. This campaign would not
have been run without the client having sufficient confidence in the researcher, sustained over a number of years,
to go to the "edge."

The research we conducted for our client encouraged an

advertising campaign that positioned butter as a very sensuous product, almost an aphrodisiac. The advertisements titillated people. It played up the sensuality of butter. Butter was smooth, provoking the most sensual responses. Even though people recognized that butter was not healthy, the sensual message communicated through the advertising worked.

Once again, sensuality triumphed over good sense!

chapter twenty-seven

Spectators vs. Participants

We all know that sports is very, very big business. This is true at all levels, from the community to the nation, and now, globally. People are increasingly engaged in sports in many, many ways and there is an endless search to increase the public engagement with sports, from ticket sales to television, from observation and spectatorship to participation, from lottery to betting.

In the 1970s, there was only one legal way to "wager" or bet on a sporting event and that was at the racetrack. The Jockey Club of Canada had retained the advertising company Vickers and Benson, and they retained us to do their research. The problem was that attendance at the race track was diminishing and, as result, betting was falling off. In our research, we went to the race track to interview people who attended and we also did focus group interviews with people who went to races occasionally, or not at all.

In studying behaviour, it is vital to go to the source or to the site where that behaviour takes place. Alternatively, as we did with Pulse, one can recreate a complex environment where people act most naturally within the site of choice. The key is to observe, listen to and understand what people are doing.

The art of observation, listening and understanding is premised on the need to know the values that drive behaviour. Values are the guiding principles of behaviour and to affect any behaviour, whether consumer or even political behaviour, you must get at those values.

So what did we find out? What did we hear and understand? Attending a racetrack was a thrill, of course. People became engrossed by the unexpected result, the competition of the races, the drama and the intensity of the event. Also, the events are very short in time. The drama was compressed. But after a brief respite, there is always another race to come. There was a matrix of events with highly dramatic character that people found exciting over a relatively long period.

However, this was only part of the experience. Being a spectator was surely important. But there was more to it, and that was betting. By betting at a horse race you went beyond being a spectator or an observer. Your experience was enhanced, deepened. You became engaged in the event; you had something "on-the-line" and you became a participant. The entire experience became more dramatic, more intense.

Participation is a very important human value that drives a lot of behaviour. Our research explained to us that attending the racetrack and betting made people not only spectators but also participants. Our research was then used by Vickers and Benson to develop an advertising campaign. The campaign was built around the phrase "Come out and be part of a horse race." It worked.

Why? Our research and its conclusions allowed us to understand two different human values and to bundle them into one slogan. The slogan encouraged people to expand their experience by being spectators and participants at the same time, at one site – the racetrack.

Today, of course, the world of betting and wagering has expanded enormously. It is now extended, legally, to many venues and sites. It encompasses sports of all sorts all around the globe. It is transforming spectators into engaged participants. There are now many other sites to engage people in the world of betting and wagering. But the fundamental experience of spectatorship, coupled with the value of participation through betting, seems to be a very effective and irresistible bundle of human values – to be exploited by many.

chapter twenty-eight

A Culture in Transition
The Challenge of Understanding

One of the seminal events of the end of the 20th century was the fall of the Berlin Wall in 1989.

Ford had been operating in Europe for many years, and, of course, when the Wall came down, it was clear that there was an opportunity to move into the Central and Eastern European market. We had been conducting research for Ford in Western Europe for many years. Our new challenge was how to understand the "new" marketplace and to market successfully in that territory?

We organized a Pulse in Hamburg, formerly part of West Germany, but we brought East Germans from Leipzig to the Hamburg Pulse. We also wanted to understand how they thought, how they behaved, what their values were? Of course, we wanted to know how to sell Fords to them. But there was a larger challenge awaiting us.

We gave each person who came to the Hamburg Pulse 100 DMs. The Leipzig participants had some extra time to spare. We told them that they could go out and do whatever they wanted with the money. We asked them to come back and participate in the Pulse and to let us know what they did with this newfound money.

Money, of course, has more than a utilitarian function – or at least that is the way we Western consumers understand it. But for people in many parts of the world, money has one only function – survival. Discretionary money, or "spending" money, so much part of our culture, does not exist for many people.

The men went off to the sex shops and explored this aspect of Hamburg. The women went off and bought consumer items. The men, clearly, had both a curiosity and an appetite for this exploration of freedom, the freedom of sexual choice and the open marketplace for sex. The women expressed their freedom to choose by purchasing goods, consumer items. When given discretionary funds for the first time, East Germans chose self-expression!

This was an intriguing piece of research. We wanted to know what the newfound "freedom" would mean to East Germans. If you give people freedom, how can they learn how to handle it? Is it innate or is it learned behaviour?

The Hamburg Pulse showed us that these people approached the car marketplace with a primary value. They fell in love with and chose cars that looked good, that were pretty, that stood out! They noticed, admired and fell in love with style. Remember the standard of East Germany...the Trabant...one shape, one style, one standard colour. Given choice, these people chose with their eyes. They wanted cars with exceptional design, with outstanding colours, with visible features. It was all shape and colour for them. It was as if they chose by making a choice based on fashion – how it looked and how it stood out in a crowd. Looking for design in products, including cars, was how they defined their individuality, how they expressed their freedom.

Clearly, design influences choice. But we learned that the first encounter with choice was driven by the value of standing out – how the car looked. Choice was making a statement about individualism; you stake out a position for yourself based on shape, style and colour and you call out, look at me! You want to be noticed by others. Design was individuality.

Of course, in the marketplace, there are other values that can influence and determine choice, such as quality. But the Ford Hamburg Pulse provided the insight as to how to market in a new marketplace. Ford was very successful in penetrating into the East German market by appealing to the new consumers' desires for design and colour. Falling in love was the key driver for choice, not knowing about the car.

However, as we know, the more people know, the more likely it is that they base their choice on quality. But people must equip themselves to know. Knowing is not instantaneous. Loving is about "falling in love." It happens quickly, almost instantaneously. But knowing requires preparation, acquiring information, learning and more.

Over time, in a mature marketplace, there is always a balance in consumer choice, a balance between knowing and loving. But our research in East Germany affirmed our view that loving comes first. However, to sustain a market position, a product must find that fine balance between quality and design, knowing and loving.

Our experience in Hamburg also made us sensitive to the challenges of cross-cultural marketing. How do you market a product, the same product, in different cultures? What adjustments are required? What kind of understanding is required?

The question can be posed differently. If values are the guiding principles of behaviour, can you find the same values in many different cultures? And, can you use the same values for marketing cars cross-culturally, because, it is values that influence behaviour?

From many decades of doing research in the automobile sector across many cultures, we would argue that there are some values, regardless of culture or country that are fundamental in consumer choices. Are there any cross-cultural values that are absolutely crucial in this market? First, today, frugality is a cross-cultural value. People want value for money. They want to know that their purchase is based on a trust between the manufacturer and the consumer. They want to know that they are getting the very best value for their hard-earned money. But frugality is not just an attribute of the consumers' choice. It must also be an attribute of the product. That translates itself into good or exceptional gas consumption. People care about the price of gas. People also think of frugality as an attribute of their vehicle that links them, as consumers and purchasers, into a global concern with frugality.

Quality is another key cross-cultural value. People want quality, because they know that quality is the hallmark of good and successful products and companies. They want cars, for example, that don't break down – cars that last a long time. They want cars to be reliable, dependable. If you combine frugality with quality, you get the three key attributes of a quality product or DQR: durability, quality, reliability.

A third important cross-cultural value that guides behaviour in the marketplace, but also in other aspects of human behaviour is family. The value of family is a key trigger for many aspects of human behaviour. In vehicles, it drives into the demand for safety. In politics, it drives into a package of values that imply truth, reliability, concern, generosity, future-orientation and a lot more.

The critical point is that in all our research, it is the search and the understanding of fundamental values that open the door to explanation of behaviour. And, of course, because marketing is a force for change, if you want to use it to change human consumer behaviour, you must understand those values.

In a globalizing world, cross-cultural marketing is becoming increasingly important. And our research shows that basic, fundamental values are becoming more similar. From North America to Europe, from Mexico to China, people care about family, durability, quality, reliability, frugality, safety and transparency. Further, with the global reach of communications, these values are taking a firmer hold in many more cultures.

Today, good design sells in every culture. It may begin locally, but if it works, if it "clicks," it becomes diffused globally and very quickly. Because these values leave deeper footprints in more cultures, the corollary is that people want to be loyal to products. If the product is imbued with the correct values, then a strong bond or loyalty between the consumer and the product is forged.

This is the covenant of affinity. It has a global reach.

chapter twenty-nine

Marketing Hard Liquor
Two Strategies
- - - - - - - -

Upscale Competition

The rules surrounding the advertising of hard liquor in North America have been very strict. Until very recently, there has been a prohibition on television and radio advertising of liquor in North America. Print is admissible, but other media advertising were restricted.

The sale of liquor, like all consumer products, is very competitive. There is an entire culture of liquor consumption. Branding is the key to liquor marketing. How to understand that culture? How to gain a competitive advantage in that marketplace?

In the 1970s, we were retained by Hiram Walker. Their brand was Canadian Club, but the dominant brand in the marketplace at that price level was the Seagram's brand V.O. Seagram's had another very successful brand in the market, Crown Royal, which was priced higher and was an older, more luxury Canadian whisky. With both brands Seagram's seemed to have a competitive advantage over Canadian Club.

Cliff Hatch Jr. was the president of Hiram Walker. He discussed with us the possibility of introducing a new brand of Canadian whisky into the market that would compete directly with Crown Royal. Was this a good idea? Could it possibly succeed? Was it right for Hiram Walker?

We recommended that the competitive package should be prepared. We would test the package. In addition, we tested many versions of the product itself with focus groups. Finally, after testing both the package and the contents, we thought we had a competitive product, which was launched into the marketplace. We went up against the undisputed dominant player and product at the high end of the Canadian whisky market, Seagram's Crown Royal. The product was called Canadian Club Classic. It proved to be successful when launched and to this very day. Hiram Walker now had a product, a competitive product, to compete with Crown Royal.

What was the lesson? First, it is always necessary to understand the competitive nature of the marketplace – who are the players, how are they positioned, why are they successful? Second, with the example of Crown Royal, we understood the power of prestige in the marketing of upscale products. Crown Royal looked prestigious. It still does. The bottle design makes it look different. It was put into a deep purple semi-velvet pull-bag that made this product look classy! It was marketed as the best there is in the marketplace. Third, we understood that the brand success of Crown Royal had a positive impact on Seagram's V.O.

Although not as prestigious, Crown Royal pulled it along in the marketplace and created brand recognition for it.

We developed an understanding about how the marketplace worked; we analyzed the Seagram's products and created a new product to go up against Crown Royal. By placing Canadian Club Classic into the prestige market category, Canadian Club also benefited.

Bar Placement

Our research in the liquor market took us into another site where we had to study human behaviour. And sites for research can be quite unique and special. We conducted hundreds of studies for Hiram Walker around the world. A few stand out. One such study is outlined here.

We were retained by John New who was the president of Corby Distillery, a subsidiary of Hiram Walker. Corby Distillery was a well-established and successful company in Corbyville, Ontario, near Kingston. They built a successful business distilling and selling rye whisky, but most of it was in bulk. The research question was to probe into the interface between the consumer and the dispensers of liquor. People could buy bottles, but much of the success or the failure of this marketing was dependent on the way other non-bottle purchasers of Canadian whisky interfaced with whisky products. The sites, clearly, were bars. It was there that people bought whisky, of all sorts. How did bars function? How did this site of human behaviour actually work? Who frequented bars? Who served at bars? How were products positioned at these bars?

We went to San Francisco and interviewed bartenders. Many of them were gay and much of the clientele at bars in San Francisco at the time were also gay. We quickly learned that to achieve success, products had to be placed in bars and bartenders would help customers choose specific products. This was called "bar call." Certain products were more prominently displayed at the bar. Bartenders would make recommendations and advise customers to drink certain brands. Some people would ask for specific brands, say Canadian Club, rather than rye whisky. Or some people would ask for a certain brand of scotch, rather than "a scotch."

We learned that bar call was real and was also worth a lot of money in the industry. Certain brands were sold at a high premium. We had to figure out how this specific market functioned. There was a unique culture at work here. Gay men had money and spent it where they felt at home and comfortable. Consumers like to feel comfortable and they tend to congregate in places where they feel themselves to be part of the community. Bars are places where certain kinds of people congregate. How to gain attention and position our products in these special marketplaces and how to get bar call? How to get your brand called? How do the gatekeepers, the bartenders, work? How to get brand placement in these bars?

We learned that the gay community had their own magazines and their own banking institutions. The community had a structure and a distinctive communications network. To influence behaviour in that community, you had to advertise and communicate in specific media. A specific story-telling strategy had to be developed and targeted at the audience and, by extension, to the bars and from there out to the community at large.

There were two other absolutely critical sites or cities where you had to achieve success in bar call in order to create a successful brand of whisky. And those were New York and Miami. You had to get bar placement in the bars of those cities to increase volume for your whisky brand.

The lesson was that to market a product successfully, you had to unearth the point or place of interaction between the consumer and the product – the site of encounter. By doing so, we had to understand the specific nature of the community that was uniquely positioned there, both as bartenders and customers. We had to track down their means of communication and get the right stories or advertising out, targeted at that community.

This, of course, raises the major question of how does a particular segment of society function? How do you influence consumer behaviour in that segment? And how does that segment influence and interact with the overall society? How does an industry relate to that segment of society? How do you sway the gatekeepers or the influencers in that segment of society?

I conducted personal in-depth interviews with bartenders. What I learned was eye-popping, fascinating, not only regarding how bartenders influenced brand selection but also how the gay community, because of discrimination, developed their own institutions, banking, real estate, grocery stores and other consumer goods. They created a world within a world in order to avoid discrimination. It was these people who had enormous influence on brand selection. Understanding them was an important component in developing the brand strategy.

The key for us was to go to the site where specific consumer behaviour was taking place. Then talk, listen, listen and observe. We discovered the unique behaviours and also the unique values of that segment of society. We had to understand how influence was exercised in these sites and these segments of society. Only then could we develop a marketing strategy to influence their behaviour.

chapter thirty

Searching for the Brand Internally
The Story of Scotiabank

— — — — — — — — — — — —

This is a story about the power of internal knowledge.

When we think of brand, we frequently think of something that is present in or presented to the marketplace. We think of a commodity, a product — something that is out there that has recognition in the public consciousness!

Branding, however, is a complex process and in some cases it emerges from an internal assessment of an organization or a company. In effect, the brand is within the organization. It must be sought out, given shape and character and then, after this process, it can be projected externally.

Goldfarb Consultants was retained by Scotiabank. Our task was to assist our client in searching out a unique brand to position it more effectively in the marketplace. Scotiabank was already a very well-established and major bank both in Canada and internationally. Yet, it wanted to undertake a reassessment and a reassertion of its brand in the marketplace. In effect, it wanted to rebrand itself in order to improve performance, recognition and gain market share.

To do this we suggested a study of the behaviour of the

various management tiers in the organization. We did not want to go outside to study perceptions external to the organization. Rather, we believed that the primary task was to study the behaviour of the organization internally. What were they trying to do, or what did they think they were trying to do internally? Would the clarification of values internal to the organization give us clarity as to how to rebrand the organization externally?

With our assistance, Scotiabank understood that a brand for an established company is often discovered internally rather than created and imposed. It learned that a business often is what it is and the process of clarification internally can be most helpful in repositioning it in the marketplace. No doubt, certain aspects of the final brand promise may be aspirational. Other aspects may be minimized, tweaked and adjusted.

Branding, however, is overwhelmingly about clarity of purpose. A brand is a promise. It is based on values. It requires disciplined execution in order to succeed. In the case of Scotiabank, our task was to define the brand, refine the process of clarification of the brand promise and assure that the brand made it clearly different from other banking institutions. The final step was to develop the strategy internally within the organization and to assure its implementation in the marketplace consistently over time.

For our assignment, it was important to leverage all sources of internal knowledge and insight. All business units in the organization had to be engaged and their voices had to be heard. Everybody within the organization had a stake in the process in order for the new strategy to succeed.

We began by organizing an internal cross-functional team of bank executives. All major units were involved. The team met diligently over a period of months. Each meeting had a specific agenda. Specific brand exercises were presented, evaluated, assessed and scrutinized. The internal process was often heated, provocative and very serious. Everybody understood the end result and believed that it would have a lasting impact on the organization.

To develop a brand, to define the promise, there must be a commitment to values. Values are guiding principles for behaviour. The brand, therefore, was not only something to present to the public and in the marketplace, but it also required internal commitment. It required people to understand the values that defined the organization and make them the guiding principles for their own behaviour. How to get to that clarification and consensus on the values?

Various core values were proposed and put out on the table for assessment. Each value was assigned to a subgroup for careful scrutiny. Each business unit and the key stakeholders were required to discuss and refine these values. Further, they were asked to consider how to implement these values within the various business units, such as IT, HR, Training, Advertising, etc. No unit was shielded or disengaged from the exercise. A consensus had to be found.

The most important thing we discovered became the brand promise. The mission of management, the mission of the bank was to help their customers make money, which was translated into a line used today: "You're richer than you think." That promise was difficult for management to accept and get their heads around. But once they did, it defined the way forward.

The search for the core values resulted in the following list:

- *Down to earth*: sincere, respectful and practical;
- *Insightful*: deeply understand customer needs;
- *Spirited*: enthusiastic "can do" attitude;
- *Winning*: make customers financially better off; and
- *Celebratory*: proactive celebration of customers and employees.

These core values were presented to the most senior executives in the bank and adopted. The promise was translated into the slogan "You're richer than you think." Scotiabank became committed to helping customers make money and become wealthier. Every aspect of the organization adopted the appropriate strategies to enact this promise. All the advertising was wedded to communicating the brand. Consistency provoked by the brand became the hallmark of Scotiabank.

Affinity, the stage beyond branding, is to be achieved by demonstrating over time that Scotiabank delivered on its promise to assist customers to make money. Savings, services and other aspects of the organization were subsumed under the brand promise. The brand clarified the core values of the organization internally and then projected them externally. All the components of Scotiabank are driven by one concept and that concept is to "help customers make money." Scotiabank, through its brand, created a point of differentiation for itself from other banks in Canada. It defined a way of thinking and positioning itself so that others are now imitating it.

The objective is to sustain the brand over a long period of time and deliver on it so that it can achieve the stage beyond branding…affinity.

Extending
the Perspective

— — — — — — — — — — — — —

chapter thirty-one

Introduction

The central argument of the book, so far, is that affinity lies "beyond" branding. Branding was the fundamental preoccupation of marketing in the late 20th century and remains a major feature of marketing strategies in the 21st century. However, our argument is that there is a need to think beyond branding, to extend our appreciation and understanding of consumer behaviour into new areas.

The tension in much of our thinking today is between those who believe in the positive force of globalization and those who believe that globalization is destructive. That debate rages on in many circles and is likely to carry on for many decades to come. The combat between globalism and localism is not new. The role of empires as they emerged in Greek, Roman, Dutch, Spanish, Chinese and Ottoman periods launched the same debates.

What we have argued is that there are creative and enduring features of all cultures, whatever the period, whatever the historical context. One aspect of that creativity is story-telling. We have argued that the many lessons of cultural anthropology that developed through the mid-20th century can focus on how marketplaces work. We can take these lessons and concepts, from story-telling to the "communal well," and reposition them into our contemporary context to best understand certain aspects of our society. In addition, we have argued that every society, including ours, creates artifacts and totems that define and guide collective behaviour. Values are the standards of behaviour and they affect individual and group behaviour.

Significantly, we believe that there is a collective consensus in the marketplace. Sometimes it is obvious and apparent. Sometimes it is elusive and evolving. The job of the researcher and the thinker, in our view, is to anticipate, clarify and identify that collective consensus. We believe that this collective consensus is the genius of the marketplace.

In other words, people in the marketplace act out of self-interest, but that self-interest is tied to the collective consensus. That is why we believe in the genius of democracy because it is a mechanism, a vehicle if you will, that allows the ship of state to move towards that collective consensus. Yes, the collective consensus does change over time, but the marketplace is what drives us forward, always seeking to live well and better. Sometimes there are errors, and yes, as we have argued, human fallibility is built into human experience. But the corrective is the endless search for the collective consensus. It is what drives political behaviour. It is the "ethical" imperative — the endless searching for that which is better — grafted onto our behaviour in the marketplace. It is the DNA of human behaviour.

Branding is the effort to forge a lasting link between the consumer and products in the marketplace. It is complex. It involves many elements. It is also an enormously creative act. And, in exploring the vagaries of branding, we have argued that we must think beyond branding...we must think towards affinity. Affinity is the hidden magic of the collective consensus. This section of this book will explore some of the implications of our thinking in various areas. We believe that the fundamental insights and constructs of our arguments can be extended into many areas and in this section we will begin to explore some of those extensions.

Part III will extend the ideas explored in Parts I and II and reflect on the nature of corporations and organizations in the contemporary world. Part II provided us with snapshots of corporations, some global, some local, as they evolved in the marketplace over past decades. Chapter 32 will build on the insights and lessons learned from those snapshots.

Chapter 33 will argue that there is, indeed, a Canadian political brand. There is a way of thinking about Canada that defines its past character and present circumstances and that can link the Canada we know to the collective consensus experienced and appreciated by most Canadians. Politics always requires reconstruction and there is a need for it at this critical juncture in Canadian history, as the Canadian nation evolves. Based on our analysis of branding and affinity, we provide some avenues for consideration.

Chapter 34 returns to a case-study approach to examine the present condition of Toyota and Ford during the current period of turmoil and market volatility. How do brands respond to crisis? Can brands sustain affinity when they suffer adversity?

Chapter 35 explores the intersection of the globalization of consumerism with the fate of democracy. We now live in an age of significant transformations in the way private lives intersect with public life. The evolution of social networks signals significant changes in how the consumer market-place works and also how politics and political influence is exercised, or may be exercised.

chapter thirty-two

The Unforgiving Public
Corporate Responsibility and Global Citizenship

- -

"Transparency is not mysterious . . . it is obvious."

Marketing and democracy are based on trust. The collective consensus that permeates the marketplace is premised on the notion that choice empowers people to act in their own self-interest, but that self-interest leads to a collective consensus. This means that there is a consensus, not anarchy. The collective consensus may take time to evolve, but this notion that choice coalesces around a product, or a politician or a party, is fundamental to the way the marketplace and the democratic marketplace works.

The power of consumerism seems now to permeate almost all societies and countries. The nature of consumerism drives one into the marketplace and affects the behaviour endemic to the marketplace. This in turn forges links between people and consumers in making choices. This is not just the contemporary hallmark of democratic politics but it also defines the nature of corporate competition.

Often, in the political world, like in the consumer

world, there is no consensus. We find fierce competition where there is no winner, no loser, and no obvious consensus. Yet, the competitive exercise is what refines and also helps define both products and politicians.

The endless process of competition in both the consumer world and in the political world endemic to the democratic process has many consequences. Competition may force one to engage in the process of renewal. However, renewal frustration may lead to passivity or even boredom. Both may well be endemic to the human condition. We learn quickly that we live with expectations, many of which have no justification. Just because we assume something, does not mean that it will always be the case. Expectations allow stability. They provide us with the absence of surprises. Not experiencing earthquakes, or the collapse of the stock market, does not ensure that it will not happen.

In the political and in the consumer marketplace, we learn very quickly that choice is fickle, or is often incomprehensible, or unexpected. We learn that choice is continuous and almost never ending. What to do, what to eat, what to think, what to...? To win over those who choose, we must always renew their interests, capture their awareness. Awareness leads to choice. The endless search for renewal is what maintains public interest in the political and consumer marketplace. It is also what drives the endless efforts for corporations and producers to renew themselves, to recreate themselves, to redefine themselves. Just as in politics where leaders must renew and recreate themselves to be successful, in the corporate world, success comes to those who can renew themselves and recreate themselves. Politicians and their parties and corporations and their products must constantly keep the public's interest, to avoid disappointment, loss of interest or rejection by the fickle process of public choice.

It is worth asking – why do companies or parties, or products and political leaders get into trouble? What is the process by which the public gets turned off? How does the consensus in the marketplace get fragmented, or disappear, or stagnate?

What drives choice? Choice is always based on self-interest, whether it is in the political marketplace or the commercial marketplace.

In a democracy where there is always a search for the collective consensus, one may well ask the question – how does one make allies, not enemies? Allies allow one to build the collective consensus, to find the route to success. Enemies provoke the disintegration of that collective consensus in the marketplace that leads to failure. Allies are bound by shared values; values forge links between people or groups who may well be different on other dimensions, such as age, religion, income, etc. Values, the standards of behaviour, are the building blocks of ally-making, the creation of the collective consensus. What is true about making allies and not enemies in politics is also true about the commercial marketplace.

Branding is about creating the bond that links the product to the consumer. Beyond branding lies affinity – the covenant that is the enduring and lasting aspect of branding. It is the ceramic content of the process of branding, the element that can withstand the vagaries of time, place, transition and more.

Affinity, as we have argued, is all about trust, long-term. Affinity is the consequence of branding. It assumes trust, the making of allies, and the avoidance of enemies. It is all about the proclamation – "Come to my side...you will be happy, you will be with the winners, you will avoid disappointment, you will know what to expect and we will always deliver on the brand promise."

There are some values that seem to be the fundamental foundations for branding and that provoke affinity. Some of those enduring values are safety, quality, family, reliability and beauty. Successful brands tap into those values and are able to renew their product lines based on those values.

Probably, in the past, there was no stronger and enduring value than quality. You could not lose with quality, either in the marketplace or in life. But if quality is the building block of enduring value, branding and affinity, the collapse of quality is the undoing of branding and affinity. Therefore, there is an obsession in the corporate world with the preservation and assurance of quality in product development, design and production.

The most telling recent example of the "test" of quality is the story of Toyota – a company and a brand dedicated to quality established over many decades. But, in a brief period, when the priorities of global growth and profit superseded the value of quality, the brand suffered immensely!

Toyota is worth studying for many reasons. They had a clearly and deliberated constructed brand, established over many years – the bull's eye at the core of their being! They adhered to clearly defined values of *kaizen* and *genchi genbutsu*. They adjusted their attributes, consistent always with their values and brand promise. They did create affinity between the brand and its public. They became a global brand, producing quality automobiles around the world in 142 plants. Regardless of their location, country, workforce, weather...whatever, the plants produced global products, clearly attached to the Toyota brand.

What made Toyota great was that they never rushed product development. Their DNA was to build the best-quality product possible...to push the bar further and further up to the next level of quality. They always succeeded in raising that bar higher and higher to differentiate themselves from the competition. That is how they led. They set the standards. Their competition took notice. The public noticed and came to them in overwhelming numbers, enough to make it the world's largest auto manufacturer in 2009.

Then, something happened...the Toyota Way became usurped by different values. Ceaseless global expansion, the pursuit of high profits, squeezing and compromising on product development set in. Quality, the hallmark of the promise, fell to second place. This happened also, in part, because of a creeping culture of infallibility.

In the consumer world, as in the political world, one must never forget that there is a public wisdom. There is a wisdom that emanates from the street. At first it may appear to be vague, but over time, it takes a shape. It is almost like osmosis, a slow seepage upwards. The ultimate power of the consumer is the power to say no, to reject either a product or a politician.

The street was telling Toyota that there was a problem with the gas pedal and the brakes. Toyota asserted its infallibility. The complaints persisted. Toyota acted arrogantly, dismissing the messages from the consumer, the experience from the street. Finally, finally, Toyota admitted the problem. Can its admission salvage the brand? Or has sufficient damage been done to the brand that quality is now compromised?

The recent Toyota experience asserts that there is a global consumer culture taking shape. The experience of Toyota drivers in the United States was echoed and replayed by Toyota drivers in Europe and Japan, and more. They found the same problems in the Toyota global product. The problem was not limited to one market. The trouble was dispersed globally!

The consumers today are better prepared than ever before. They have more access to information; they share their knowledge. Information in the consumer marketplace gets diffused very quickly, at almost viruslike speed. Raw impressions are shared, sometimes without being fully substantiated. It is also important to remember that the new consumer in the United States is not just informed but also litigious. Class action suits are the norm. Taking on Goliath is commonplace. Tobacco fell, and then pharmaceuticals, and now even Toyota has slipped up.

Toyota underestimated the preparedness of the consumer. They did not understand how well prepared the consumer had become. Today, knowledge is, indeed, power. It is not limited to experts. Consumer knowledge is now available and shared globally.

The consumer confronted Toyota and asserted that no company, not even Toyota, can take risks at the expense of their customers. Toyota tried to compromise on quality. They were found out. They were revealed and punished globally, not just in one market.

Toyota's first reaction was arrogant; they tried to deny, then they tried to hide, then they blamed the consumer, and then they were forced to admit there was a problem. Finally, after all else failed, they apologized and came clean.

Global companies and all companies must now face the new consumer. The lessons from the recent Toyota story must be absorbed. Global companies in terms of their own internal culture must place consumer protection as their primary value. There cannot be any secrets; there is no place to hide. If you are not transparent, you cannot be successful any longer. Every email is a public document. The virus of information, especially if it is bad news, moves very quickly and can infect everybody and everything.

Globalization means that companies today must be proactive not just to protect themselves, but to protect the consumer. The new consumer is informed and also litigious. How can companies behave in this new environment?

Major companies, such as Toyota, now think globally. Historically, such companies, from the Hudson's Bay Company to the East India Company, from Ford to Toyota, believed that their internal culture could allow them to compete internationally or globally and succeed. One can study these companies from that perspective, namely, how they developed an internal corporate culture that then became globalized as their operational model. With the fall of Toyota from grace, this may no longer be sufficient as an operational model for a global company.

Many factors are now at play in the global marketplace. First, the consumer is now not only a consumer of global products produced by global companies, but also a global consumer, fully aware of the character the global product and also fully knowledgeable of the global producer. It may have been humbling for the CEO of Toyota, Mr. Toyada, to be called on the carpet and to be obliged to appear before a Congressional committee in Washington, DC. But it was in metaphorical terms an international tribunal driven by US consumers and owners of Toyota products calling Toyota, this global corporate giant, to account for its failures.

This is a new reality. There are global consumers driven by primary values, such as safety in the Toyota case, but also by a deep sense of injustice and grievance, who can force a global company to account for itself. Ironically, of course, the "mock trial" was held in the United States where the customer is king and where the marketplace is the locus of judgment, in products and also in politics. The empowerment of the consumer and the consequences for the conduct of producers in the competition for products and success in this fierce marketplace is, indeed, enormous.

The Toyota story has revealed that a huge gap exists between the producers of global products and their understanding of this new global consumer culture. Toyota first denied the validated experience of the consumer but was then forced to admit there was a problem and it tried to fix the problem. It was forced to recognize and admit that the consumer was right.

The second new reality is that knowledge is readily available. Major companies may deny facts; they may choose to discard personal experience, but the free flow of information, the ability to document personal experience and to disseminate that experience to an attentive audience directly though the new social networks means that personal experience now is not just personal, but personal experience can become global. The Toyota consumer in Abu Dhabi, or

Beijing, or Rio became fully cognizant about the problems at Toyota, not by public disclosure by the producer but by personal exposure and verification by individuals, like themselves, originating at first in the United States but recognizable in Europe, Asia, everywhere.

Consumers can now share their brand experiences directly with other consumers, unmediated by the media, by corporate disclosure or anything else. Personal verification authenticated by posting such experiences on the Internet is now the most powerful mechanism of public disclosure. People share their own experiences and, most significantly, others use this disclosure to seek information or to authenticate their experiences. Before they enter into the marketplace to make a choice and a decision, they now ask others, people like you, directly, "What do you think, what was your experience with this product?"

Knowledge is, of course, power. People believe each other. They can now tell each other their own stories, expose their own experiences, unmediated by third parties. Here is where the "truth" now resides. The marketplace of unmediated knowledge and experiences resides in Wikipedia, Twitter and Facebook.

The consumer culture, indeed, has now changed. And one may well begin thinking not only of global products produced by global companies for a global marketplace, but also of a global consumer culture. This culture is very much alive, defining itself continuously, authenticating its own experiences, endlessly abuzz with stories, sharing personal experiences, evaluating products, assisting everybody in making their choices and decisions in the marketplace.

Toys with toxic paint produced in China masquerading as global products are unacceptable to the emerging global consumer culture. Retooled, mutant seeds developed by Monsanto are being contested as legitimate global products in this new robust global consumer culture. The new global consumer culture is now flexing its muscles in the debate on environmentalism. Other products are next.

This new global consumer culture is being discovered in many countries by politicians and political parties. There is a recognition that the marketplace is now much more "layered" than before, with many more vehicles of influence operating simultaneously. Advertising remains important, but within the ever-expanding universe of interactivity, other forms of influence and interaction are taking shape and expanding very, very, very quickly. This is the new reality of consumers and their behaviour in the competitive marketplace; this is the new reality of the restructured marketplace.

Another way of thinking about this, of course, is to think about the marketplace historically. People would gather around the village well to communicate, to tell their stories, to hear others' stories, to get the news, perhaps to engage in the exchange of products. The village well then became commercialized and was organized for the exchange of commercial products. The market emerged.

That marketplace moved from a local focus, to a regional focus to a national focus to an international focus. Finally, today, products and production are co-mingled with the globalization of the consumer market. We even have developed regulations to enhance the free development and free flow of products in the global marketplace. Everybody, everywhere, or almost everybody, everywhere, wants in and has bought into it.

The global consumer through new vehicles of communication had honed in on an emerging systemic problem at Toyota. Toyota was unmasked as having betrayed its own corporate culture. This was the true story of humbling the giant. The new global consumer forced the CEO to admit that the fundamental values of the company had been betrayed internally. The failure was not just mechanical, nor in engineering nor in computerization. The failure was a betrayal of the values of the company itself and the responsibility had to be fixed internally. Everybody within the company, including the CEO, was guilty of betraying the brand promise and the values of the company.

We have argued that values are guiding principles for behaviour. Values are contained within a culture; they are the DNA of a culture. Global companies, over many decades, develop their own internal cultures, their own DNA. They become guided by and also captives of their own values. The Toyota story is an epic story of a great company that has been betrayed internally. It was through the efforts of the new global consumer that this story revealed itself.

Toyota is now cognizant of a new reality. There are indications that others are becoming aware, as well. There are some indications that China seems to appreciate this new global consumer culture as it tries to retool much of its productive capacities to satisfy the demands of the new global consumer. Toxic paints on children's toys are wrong. Food products produced for the global market must meet the demands and the expectations of an informed global consumer. All products produced for the global marketplace and for the global consumer must live up to international standards of safety, health, security and environmentalism. Quality now has acquired a deeper meaning.

Can one begin to outline a different code of conduct for global companies in the new context of a robust, alert, informed global consumer? What could be the primary values to govern global companies?

We have argued that beyond branding lies affinity. Companies that endure must create an epoxy, a bond, between the product and the consumer. That best product emerges from companies that clearly define their own character. Affinity emerges from companies with clear personalities and that radiate values important to the consumer. We have argued that this is not only true in the commercial marketplace, but also in the political marketplace.

We have also argued that fallibility is a positive value. Mistakes and failure are endemic to the human enterprise, commercial and political. To retain affinity, to protect a brand, fallibility and the recognition of human error may be humbling, but necessary. In the automobile sector, recalls are quite common. They can be absorbed by the public and they may not be damaging to a brand if there is both recognition of error and humility, as well as a desire to correct the error.

The fundamental value consumers now demand is transparency. People want the truth, they do not want secrets. They want and demand the "goods," not obfuscation and avoidance. They want the truthful news — even if the news may not be great!

Another way to make the argument is that avoidance is recognizable and provokes aggressive inquiry. People smell avoidance. Their sixth sense tells them when a politician is not telling the truth, or when a company is avoiding the obvious. The consumer wants to see into a product, a producer or a politician. They want to know everything about a product and its claims or assertions. Or, we as consumers are very clever about knowing the personality in front of us, whether it's a commercial product or a politician.

It is hardly a wonder that we are so attentive. Every day, from morning to night, everybody of every age, from childhood to old age, is constantly being asked to make choices and decisions. We do so from the most mundane to the most complex of choices. This is what the marketplace teaches us — how to discriminate, how to make decisions in our own self-interest. The marketplace is, indeed, the litmus paper test of acceptability. Over time, in the marketplace, a collective consensus emerges where certain products or politicians pass the test or do not.

Today, we demand to know more and more about the product or the politician. We demand transparency. That is what the new global consumer is constantly looking for and demanding. What is behind this? Where does it come from? What will it do for me? How well can I know it? No secrets...do not deceive me, I want to have confidence not just in the product and the process, but I also want to have confidence in the personality and character of the productive process.

The solution to these demands is the need to elevate transparency as a primary value both in the productive process and in the political process. No hidden tricks, no private secrets, no lying...we can and will find you out! We will force you to come clean! We will reveal the truths, whether it is through a Congressional committee in the United States, the Gomery Commission in Canada or the International War Crimes Tribunal in The Hague.

We all have a human propensity to try to keep secrets. From a young age on, we like secrets, we like whispers, we try to share our secrets as an act of absolute confidence only with those we trust. It seems as if all cultures have this propensity to secrecy. The line between the public and the private runs very, very deep.

The new forms of social networking seem to be changing that line, or at least shifting it. What used to be appropriately revealed about the self in a private and secretive diary now is put on the "wall" on Facebook. Revealing your own very private self seems to be increasingly acceptable. The concept of privacy is being eroded – what was once private is no longer. Or, people are beginning to feel much more comfortable with aspects of transparency. We learn and train ourselves now increasingly in this marketplace.

Global companies and their own internal culture must now recognize that there is a new value pertinent in this global consumer world and that they must integrate this demand for transparency into their own DNA.

There is, however, a further consequence emerging from the new reality of an informed, savvy, interconnected global consumer culture. Transparency emerges as a response to a new set of demands emerging from the globalized consumer marketplace. In one sense, it is an obligation imposed on global brands and global producers in order to retain credibility in the competitive global marketplace.

Yet, it goes further. The global consumer now demands to be protected from untruth, the shirking of responsibility, from avoidance, from defects that can lead to accident or even deaths. The internal culture of global companies now must incorporate not just telling the truth when asked, or probed or demanded of them. Those are reactive instincts or modes of operating. The pro-active component or value is volunteering to tell all, volunteering to come clean. Transparency may well be a response to the possibility of both being challenged and being penalized for non-disclosure.

However, the pro-active value is voluntarism, doing something not because of an analysis or fear of consequence, but because it is, in itself, the correct and ethical thing to do. It is right in itself.

Transparency is what maintains brand equity. If you want your brand to work and to create affinity for your product in the marketplace, you need to have global values. In the new global consumer marketplace, as we are quickly learning, transparency is required. You do not keep secrets from one market because of the interconnectivity of all markets.

The corollary of this is to endorse voluntarism as a new corporate value. Voluntarism is the antidote to secrecy. It is the logical consequence of transparency because it is acting pro-actively. Voluntarism can become a powerful corporate value. It may well be a further strategic and practical value to enhance brand equity. The consequence may well be the further enhancement of affinity, or a way of engineering affinity in the marketplace.

The empowered global consumer now is a reality. The corporate world is beginning to learn how to respond and, hopefully, embrace the new demands the global consumer is making. Transparency is one response to the unfolding drama provoked by Toyota. A new corporate ethic of voluntarism may be another whereby the company can reach out to the new global consumer.

Altruism, the unselfish concern with the welfare of others and the giving of benefit or resources to others, has been an aspect of corporate culture in many places. The arts and culture communities have benefited from many altruistic acts. McDonald's pushed this further and created many Ronald McDonald homes, thereby creating positive affect and perception of its corporate culture. Many corporations try to align themselves with community groups, public goods, charities, foundations and more.

Voluntarism may be the going beyond altruism, pushing the corporate culture into many new areas. To embrace the new savvy consumer, companies will be wise to graft into their operational systems modalities of voluntarism, whereby they willingly give discriminating global public information, resources, values and more. Perhaps, public companies will need to have board committees to deal with the new ethics of transparency and voluntarism in order to protect their shareholders and their equity.

Beyond branding lies affinity. The emerging struggle in the competitive global marketplace is to engineer affinity. Branding is a process that we have explored and explained. The new discovery of the robust global consumer and the drama at Toyota may well give us insight into the territory beyond branding...affinity!

chapter thirty-three

Branding and Affinity in Politics
The Just Society
-- -- -- -- -- -- -- -- --

Politics is both process and vision. Success in politics is a combination of the two. Vision alone will not lead to continued success. Vision becomes the guide for public policy. In order to achieve results in politics, one must be a master of process. Good public policy means conjoining vision with a mastery of process.

The search for vision in politics is continuous, but achieved infrequently. In Canada, the apogee of this vision in politics was the definition of the "Just Society" by Pierre Trudeau in 1968. It was a concept that drove everything else.

Trudeau introduced this concept to Canadians in 1968 in order to define himself and to define the country. By this concept alone, he found a way to define Canadian values and both define and invigorate the Canadian psyche. The concept gave Canada a sense of self-pride and clarified the very essence of the nation. Canadians got on-board with him in 1968. During a period of 16 years, from 1968 to 1984, through five elections, Canadians experienced a unique brand of politics that was different from previous political regimes. It was a period, indeed, of brand politics. It was distinctive, quite special and it gave the Liberal Party of Canada a definitive brand.

What was the brand?

At the core of the brand was a bull's eye, a promise of performance and a definition of intent and vision. It was the "Just Society," a phrase crafted by Trudeau and his team for the 1968 election. Remember the "Great Society" of President Johnson in the United States? That too was a brand promise that, alas, because of a variety of circumstances did not come to fruition. But the core of the 1968 Trudeau and Liberal Party brand, the Just Society did stick. It came to define and also to propel public policy through the next 16 years of almost uninterrupted Liberal Party rule in Canada.

Often in politics, it is the turn of phrase that reverberates, that compels human behaviour and tends to stick. The discourse on justice is very ancient and has been at the centre of social and political considerations for endless centuries. Justice is a noun; it defines a quality of a person or a thing. It implies being moral, an attribute of a person or a process.

What Trudeau did was transform the noun into an adjective and joined it to society, to Canadian society. He issued a challenge to every Canadian to engage in justice, to think of themselves, their actions, the actions of their politicians, their communities, to measure every aspect of themselves and their own society against the yardstick of justice. The

Just Society became not just a challenge to be enacted, but it also became the ethical imperative for every Canadian. We were asked to build a Just Society, to engage in its construction, to be its guardians.

The Just Society allowed Liberals to know who they were and what they aspired to. From a branding perspective, it was brilliant. It was not only a promise to drive values and attributes, but it also gave government and the people of Canada a set of rules for the political game. It became the measure of performance, a very high measure of performance, but a significant one. The same way as people are able to measure the promise and the performance of Toyota relative to its brand, and, as today, it is a critical measure leading to criticism and rejection, the Just Society became the measuring stick relative to the Trudeau governments and the Liberal Party of Canada.

The term "Just Society" became the story of Canada. It became and remains an indelible part of the Canadian story and defines our very conscience. The term also forced other political parties and subsequent governments to find out and to define themselves. No government in Canada or political party can hope to achieve success without this challenge laid down to them by the Just Society.

The Just Society also had a powerful incorporative force within it. It meant that justice had to engage everybody in society. Everybody had a stake in it, not just the courts or the government. It was an all-inclusive term. Beyond that, it meant that trust, the *sine qua non* of justice, was the responsibility of everybody — individuals, communities, society and governments. The collective consensus that is the genius of democracy is premised on this shared sense of trust. Trust is mutual, not one-way. The people elect their representatives to enact the collective consensus on their behalf. In turn, trust must be reciprocated between the government, the representatives and the people. The mutuality of trust is binding. No hidden agendas, no secrets...debate, discord, yes, but trust implies transparency and openness.

The Just Society reverberated in Canada because it both reflected the Canadian experience and also set out a brand promise. Canadian history was premised on the fact that the conquerors trusted the conquered to live peaceful and just lives within their own institutions, religion and laws and with their own language. That was the consequence of 1760 and Confederation. No brutal transformations, no prerogatives of power and the powerful. Minorities count, a process of respect and trust was enshrined.

The Just Society as a national brand promise was reinvigorated and renewed by bold moves such as multiculturalism. The respect for minorities, to trust strangers to become your neighbours and your equals, to tolerate difference and embrace difference as a measure of generosity and a test of respect...all became part of the Just Society.

In our analysis of branding, values, the second ring of the bull's eye, envelop and give substance, direction and content to the brand promise. The third circumference delineates the attributes of the brand. At the core of the brand is the vision that radiates or illuminates throughout the three concentric circles of the brand.

Just Society

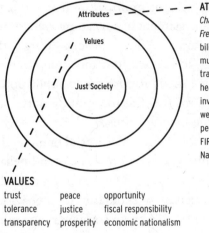

ATTRIBUTES
Charter of Rights and Freedoms
Freedom of Information Act
bilingualism
multiculturalism
transfer payments
health care
investment in education
welfare and employment insurance
peacekeeping
FIRA
National Energy Policy

VALUES

trust	peace	opportunity
tolerance	justice	fiscal responsibility
transparency	prosperity	economic nationalism

The values that circumscribed the Just Society include justice and peace, transparency, tolerance and trust, economic nationalism, prosperity and opportunity. Each one of these values constitutes the building blocks of the Just Society and propelled details of public policy and political decision-making. These are the guiding standards for behaviour that guide policy. None can contradict the promise of the brand – the just society.

The attributes are the policies that are put into place or the measure and the practices of the government that extend the values and that reflect the brand promise. Over a period of 16 years, the outstanding attributes of the Just Society included the *Charter of Rights and Freedoms*, the *Freedom of Information Act*, bilingualism, multiculturalism, transfer payments, health care, investment in education, welfare and unemployment insurance, FIRA, peacekeeping, the National Energy Policy, to name a few. The endless search for the attributes of the brand promise drove public policy. These policies emerged from a clear recognition of the values that surrounded the brand promise.

Marketing is a force for change. A powerful brand is able to change the marketplace, to refine the values and behaviours of people. In a sense, a powerful brand resets the rules in the marketplace. It sets new standards for behaviour. Toyota did so in cars. Apple did so with computers and other electronic devices. There are many such successful brands.

The Just Society was a force for change in the manner and conduct of Canadian politics. The concept challenged our innate feelings of prejudice and redefined how we thought of ourselves, of Quebecers, of minorities, of others. The Just Society made the *Charter of Rights and Freedoms* possible and this bold act of Parliament, preceded by bilingualism and multiculturalism, redefined the notion of Canadian citizenship.

The Just Society was the enabler of many redefinitions of the manner and conduct of Canadian public policy. It challenged the existing political order and gave it a new direction. It forced the mantle of responsibility and a new civil conduct of society on everybody. It declared that henceforth, every citizen, every person in the Canadian society had to be trusted and had to be the carrier of the concept of justice. The just society was our conscience, our consciousness, our alter ego!

In thinking about a brand for a political party and a government, one must think about the relationship between the promise, the values that reflect the promise and the attributes that bring together the values in terms of public policy. Often, in brand analysis, there is a dissonance between the promise or the brand and the values or the values and attributes. What makes the analysis of the Just Society so interesting and what appears to be a lasting legacy for this brand of Liberal Party politics and also what stands out as the lasting legacy of Trudeau and the Trudeau regime in Canada is the radiation of the promise of the Just Society through the values and attributes of public policy.

The Just Society stuck as the measure of performance of the Trudeau regime. It also led to intense criticism and near electoral defeat in 1972 and electoral defeat in 1979. The electorate felt betrayed by the performance relative to the promise. In 1974, the electorate again put its faith in the Just Society as a brand promise and elected a majority Liberal government. In 1979, the electorate punished the

Liberal government because of the economy; remember, inflation was running at 23 to 24 per cent and a minority Conservative government came to power. In 1980, another Liberal majority government was elected.

The Just Society does, indeed, continue to stick as the hallmark of the Liberal Party of Canada. And, like many other brands in the marketplace, it is tested, it is contested, it is analyzed and is deconstructed. The question remains whether this brand can be reconstructed for the 21st century?

Part of the argument of this book is that we must think beyond branding. And, in doing so, we must think about "affinity." Affinity is the personality of a brand. It is the charisma of the product as it is positioned in the marketplace.

No doubt Pierre Trudeau, at least for a significant period of his political career, was not only able to imprint a brand on the Liberal Party of Canada, but also was able to create affinity between the Canadian public and himself and his party. It was recognizable, it was distinctive, it had personality and it had a unique character.

Affinity, as we have argued, is a way of bonding a listener or an audience or a consumer to a story-teller, or a product. Affinity needs a great story to be told, a story that becomes a covenant, a compact in words and deeds that define a relationship based on expectations and performance.

Every society, at all times and all places, craves for a great story-teller, or a great story. During mundane times, these great stories and story-tellers are absent. The high moments of public life or the great and historic moments of a society seem to reflect these great story-telling periods.

Stories define the character of a society. They reflect our fundamental beliefs. Stories and ideas are different. Ideas are not timeless in themselves as they tend to be grounded in particular times and places or situations. Stories, however, are forever as they are rooted deeply in the standards of human behaviour. That is why we always go back to the great stories because they tell something about ourselves, regardless of the time, place or circumstance of one's existence.

At the centre of any great story lies a concept. The power of a concept is that it drives values. Values are guiding principles for behaviour. Values are the standards we use to make judgments and choices. In public life, the public policy choices made reflect the values emitted by a regime and become the embodiment of those values, or they are the living attributes of the regime, infused in all public policies.

The Just Society and Pierre Trudeau left a huge footprint on the consciousness of the Canadian public, much like any product with affinity does in the marketplace. Affinity of a product does not always mean total market domination. Indeed, as Apple has shown, affinity of their product in a competitive marketplace does not supplant everything else. But, it provokes loyalty, recognition, distinctiveness, an indelible bonding between a public and the product, a bonding that persists for many, many years. The Just Society and Pierre Trudeau did that in Canadian politics. It created a legacy that endures in a passionate, distinctive manner, even today.

The Just Society gave Canadians an identity different from the Americans. It was a big idea based on recognition of a certain set of values. Values are guiding principles for human behaviour. Trudeau was able to provide that definition and to explicate the Canadian value system so that Canadians could identify themselves and identify with Canadian values. They could conduct their public affairs and even their communal and private comportment with a clear recognition of those values.

The Just Society became the Trudeau brand. But by crafting his own brand of leadership, he also created affinity between himself and large segments of Canadian society. His political career suffered ups and downs – remember that he won three majority governments, but he lost his majority in 1972 and in the 1979 election, he lost power. But the legacy of the Just Society remains an indelible part of Canadian society, its history and also its collective psyche.

The vision contained in the Just Society was also a guiding principle, not only for the conduct of leadership but also as translated into public policy. It defined and dictated the perspectives that contributed to health care, transfer payments, child care, the creation of Petro-Canada, the CROW rate legislation and the battle against separatism. The Just Society was a prescription for making Canada a fair place to live, a place that respected all of its citizens.

Legacy in politics is vital. In Canada, all leaders of the Liberal Party who succeeded Trudeau – John Turner, Jean Chrétien, Paul Martin, Stéphane Dion, Michael Ignatieff – had to come to grips with the political legacy of the Just Society, the Liberal Party brand. They all had to accept the challenge of translating that brand into affinity between themselves and the public. Jean Chrétien embraced the notion of the Just Society. He was the "little guy from Shawinigan" who fought for the cause of the First Nations. He was the guy with heart. He was the "little guy" who could say "no" and refused to take Canada into the American War in Iraq. Chrétien's success was built on his ability to build on the Liberal brand, to renovate it in keeping with the new times and new circumstances.

Political leaders who inherit a successful brand contained in a political party seem to have ambiguous instincts. Can they simply extend the brand or do they have to reconstruct the brand? Are they caretakers of the brand, or do they need to put their own imprint on the brand? In the marketplace, Steve Jobs was able to inherit a languishing Apple brand and to put his own imprint on it to reinvigorate it. Apple is Apple...but it is not the same Apple under Steve Jobs as it was under Steve Wozniak.

Leaders in companies do not need to rebrand the brand. You don't need to change the Ten Commandments. The covenant survives leader after leader. The brand – political or commercial – remains; however, it always needs to be adjusted, repolished or tweaked by leaders based on circumstances. Events demonstrate and define a leader. Chrétien was defined by the big event of saying "no" to the Americans on Iraq. Martin was defined by deficit fighting.

How to distinguish the personality of a political leader from the success of the brand? Is it the task of a leader, whether in product categories or politics, to refine the brand, or change the values of the brand or develop new attributes to the brand promise? What is the relationship among the brand, the values and the attributes, and how do or should leaders comprehend their own role in this equation?

Stability is based on the brand promise. People want those assurances, expectations that come from a successful brand. Values evolve very slowly in cultures. Values give things definition and foundation. They provide the guides for behaviour. The attributes of a brand, the third ring, do change based on circumstances but they are grounded in and derive from values and the brand promise.

The fine line between tradition and innovation, between inheritance and renovation, between brand and affinity, stagnation and reconstruction, both in the marketplace and in the political area is difficult, but vital. What to accept and what to reject? What to renovate and what to obliterate? Optimism is a function of core thinking. Preparation and optimism are required. That was the brilliance of the Chrétien and Martin tandem. Canadians became confident because we finally realized we could control our own behaviour. We cut the deficit and we became a nation that produced surpluses. That produced enormous confidence and optimism in our country. Of course, there were moments and periods of disquiet. But, we were told, we had to stay the course because they appealed to our values. We did. Canadians emerged optimistic, and now our success is an example to nations everywhere.

In the marketplace brands have histories. Likewise in politics. The Just Society was conceived as a template as to how people in Canada should behave and think. It is our belief structure, providing substance to what we believe. Brand experience creates memories. These memories create impact that can reverberate over a long time.

Paul Martin, the former Canadian prime minister, had a vision that in reality was defined by the Just Society. He wanted to reinvigorate the education system, the health-care system and child care. He wanted to create centres of excellence and provoke Canadian research into new fields. He had a vision of a 21st-century economy where Canada could be globally successful. He thought there was a genuine Canadian brand of thinking and acting that could be successful in a globally competitive era. He had a vision of creating global cooperation between the major and emerging economic powers, crafted into the Group of 20. Martin had all the right instincts but he could not deliver on his promised brand of Canadian politics because his thoughts were not connected to a brand promise he could articulate.

Paul Martin did change politics in Canada during his seven years as Chrétien's minister of finance. He convinced Canadians over that period of time that the new collective consensus of Canada was that deficits are wrong. Responsibility in public finances of the nation was a primary value. Martin convinced Canadians that deficits create public anxiety. Deficits are aberrations that could no longer be tolerated. He made us very conscious of the need to pay for what we want — now. Mortgaging our public finances could no longer be part of the collective consensus. People innately understood that deficits produced insecurity and deficits provoked a lack of confidence in government and even in each other. Martin convinced us that balanced budgets should be the norm. Responsibility in public finances became part of the value package of Liberal politics. He renovated the Liberal brand by attaching responsibility in public finances to the equation.

The brilliance of the Chrétien and Martin years was that it gave Canadians confidence in what they could achieve because of their self-discipline. What is unaffordable may be attractive and, indeed, we may want it. But the public appetite for public goods could only be achieved through the litmus paper test of what was affordable. Self-discipline became attached to the notion of controlling your own destiny. And Martin taught Canadians that the Canadian destiny depended on responsibility in public finances.

The genius of marketing is implementation. Having the

right concept or the right idea is necessary, but not sufficient. Martin, as leader, could not convince the public that
he was bigger than his ideas. His ideas, his policies, were
all correct in themselves. But they did not cohere, they did
not coalesce, they were devoid of a defining concept, a single vision. They were not aligned to a brand concept like
the Just Society. Martin did not articulate his ideas within
a brand promise and, therefore, they could not encompass
everybody. As a result, Martin was a political disappointment. He was quickly punished by the Canadian electorate.
After being the master of the political process as an
extraordinarily successful minister of finance for seven
years, he failed as a political leader.

Dion attempted to bring his concerns about the environment into the Liberal brand promise. He tried to build
on to the Liberal promise, to renovate it. He did not succeed
in convincing people that the renovation of the brand, as he
saw it, would give Canada a leadership role or a distinctive
point of view on the world. He failed to convince us, but
the concept was correct. Here was a leader who was elected,
had a powerful idea, but who was unable to coherently
attach this idea to a bigger idea. Dion's environmentalism
was admired, but it was never connected to the Liberal
brand or convincingly related to Liberal values. He may have
reached into the Trudeau file and argued that the environmental file should be attached to the Just Society and to
economic nationalism. He did not, and his failure to do so

is why he could not create affinity between the electorate and his Liberals.

The power of branding in politics is key. Inheritance is also key. The inheritance of the Liberal brand cannot be avoided or overlooked. In working within a brand, whether a consumer brand or a political brand, one must find the policies or the attributes to extend the brand promise, but still be true to its core.

The Just Society positioned the Liberal Party and challenged all other parties to define themselves. It was the Just Society positioning that demonstrated a void in the positioning of other parties. The other parties in Canada are searching for the big idea to wrap themselves around. They have not, as yet, found a big idea more relevant than the Just Society. Until they do, their search continues but they do not have a recognizable brand that defines the collective consensus of Canadians. Lasting and decisive political success eludes them.

Stephen Harper, the current prime minister, has his indecision, which defines him. Harper is still searching for his big idea that will establish his brand promise for himself and his Conservative Party. Without the words to describe the big idea, there will not be a way to get people to gravitate to the Conservative Party. A series of attributes unconnected to a big idea, or a brand promise, will not attract people. A series of legislative initiatives, or policies, without having a brand promise, fail to create affinity. You need the promise. Then you get coherence. Liberals, over two or more decades, positioned themselves in the shadow of the Just Society. The Tories do not yet have a positioning and, as such, their brand promise does not exist in a way that average Canadians can feel motivated and buy in to it.

The present Canadian prime minister was driven into politics from a variety of political roots in the Reform Party and in Western Canada. Those roots are also entwined with a set of political beliefs and values. But in the search for political success, Harper has tried to camouflage those values and those beliefs. Yet, those values do emerge, or erupt, often enough and seem to define him. In our analytic terms, the Conservative government of Mr. Harper is pursuing a variety of policies, or attributes, premised on a covert value system that seems to be camouflaged. Examples of this are their legislation on crime and their intention to expand the prison system, their policies on gun registration, their policies on allowing increased foreign investment and foreign takeovers of Canadian mining company giants, environmental policies, choice for women and more. Each one of these policies, or attributes, emerges from a set of values. Our analysis is to suggest a link between these policies and a clarification of those Conservative government values that appear to encompass paternalism, conservatism (resistance to change) and secrecy.

Furthermore, we would suggest that it is vital to juxtapose those values against the Canadian value system and, more clearly, to juxtapose those values against the authentic Canadian brand, namely the Just Society. This Canadian brand has evolved as the collective consensus. It is the Canadian conscience.

The Bloc Québécois has a simple but big idea – separatism. They know themselves. They have a brand, they know what they are. Their image is who they are. They know that if they cannot have it today, they will continue making the case for their brand of separatism endlessly into the future. Their values are overt because they have a core promise, a brand. This brand, however, is inconsistent with the collective consensus of Canadians.

It is worthwhile asking the same questions and doing the same analysis of the NDP. Is there a relevant, clear, discernible brand promise in the NDP today? What is their bull's eye? Are there overt values that drive their attributes and policy priorities? How does the brand promise, if there is one, relate to their past, their traditions, to the Canadian conscience and the collective consensus?

Michael Ignatieff remains a conundrum. Image is a function of what you are. You cannot change what you are fundamentally. An image can be tweaked, but you cannot recreate a person in the public space of politics. Yes, sharp edges can be smoothed. Tie and shirt can be changed. But given the endless microscope of media attention, what you are is what you get…is what comes across…is what it is. Michael Ignatieff became the leader of the Liberal Party without thinking how to put his imprint on the Liberal brand. He could have embraced the Just Society as the legacy and the brand of the Liberal Party. He shied away from that. The reasons may well be his inconsistencies of having adopted political positions too closely related to the American value system.

I believe Ignatieff's writings are his true thoughts. He is now trying to speak as if those writings never happened. The public smells that he is not transparent with them. What he wrote is what he really believes…not what he now says. There is an inconsistency between the two. We have argued that transparency is now a key global value, essential for success. Both Ignatieff and Harper seem to think they do not need to embrace it.

To be successful as the leader of the Liberal Party, Ignatieff would have to embrace the concept of the Just Society, add attributes that are pertinent and timely to it, not change the brand or the promise. He did not understand the principles of brand development. His urgent challenge is to enhance the brand of the Liberal Party. His major task is to keep the Liberal brand promise relevant today. The job is to create more affinity to the promise and the Liberal Party. You do that by developing the attributes of the brand. Ignatieff appears unwilling at this point in time to embrace the Just Society as the Liberal brand.

The search for pertinent policies that resolve a society's pressing and urgent problems is always the political challenge. That is what legislation does. That is the task of bureaucracies, under the direction of political leadership, or those in power.

However, the leadership challenge in every democracy

is to link or derive the policies from some collective consensus. Political parties in democratic societies are always trying to forge that collective consensus, to tap into it, to articulate it, to find the core, the heart, the pulse of that collective consensus. Successful political parties find a way to define that collective consensus.

The most successful such definition in Canadian politics over the past many decades was the Just Society and the Liberal Party of Canada wrapped itself around that self-definition. It became the brand of the Liberal Party and it also became the conscience of the majority of the Canadian public.

Image is what you are...not what you want to be. To be able to know a politician – the same as about knowing a product or a product line – the public wants to probe into his or her past, into their secrets. Fallibility is now endemic to truth and trust. It is true in the consumer world and also true in the political world.

To truly trust a politician, as is also true about truly trusting a product, we want the whole story; we do not want a partial truth. We send out journalists, people, spooks, to get at the truth, even the dirt. We need to know all of the warts as well as the perfections. When the public learned all about Trudeau, or Clinton, was the brand betrayed? Fallibility can make for a different kind yet an enduring affinity.

In politics, the theory of branding is key. It is building

on...not destroying and rebuilding. The theory of branding leads to the covenant. A political leader or a CEO adds to a brand. One should never forget that the promise and values are sacrosanct. They are the building blocks of a stable society.

It is often remarked that Canada during the 20th century had a dominant party, almost a single successful party. Over a century, a Liberal brand was established. It became so successful that the Liberal promise became Canada's promise. Brand promises are able to rally people around them.

In the consumer world and in the political world, brand experience is vital. People associate themselves with great and successful brands as they have done with the Liberal Party because they like the brand experience. And brand experience, in a strange way, has a memory. People relive that brand experience on a continuous basis. It is that repetitive experience that allows them to have stability, whether it is in the consumer world or the political world.

Memory is tied to stories and to great story-telling. You see the image of global brands, such as BlackBerry, Nikon, Coke, Nike, Cartier and Prada, and you recall the story, the experience and the pack of memories triggered by your past association with the brand experience. In politics, as well, the same thing happens. Political parties are storehouses of memories, experiences and associations.

The memory of the Liberal Party of Canada is absolutely tied to the great story-telling connected to the Just Society.

It is this memory, this brand experience, that impacts people. Of course, like all good brands, it must be refreshed, rekindled and renewed over time by hitching the brand to pertinent attributes that are meaningful to a new public, those attributes that are founded on a set of values.

In analytic terms, one may well ask of any political regime the same questions: What is its promise or brand? What are its values? What are its attributes? The exercise of deconstructing a political regime in these terms is very effective and brings clarity to debate and discourse.

We have argued that thinking "brand...and beyond" is helpful in the marketplace and internally within organizations. It is also helpful in the realm of politics, to political parties, political regimes or governments and in public debate. It may also be helpful for political leaders who assume the leadership mantle of a political party.

chapter thirty-four

Good Times, Bad Times, New Times?

We seem to be living in a period of enormous turmoil everywhere. Maybe we are more alert than ever before, maybe we are supersaturated with news, maybe there is, indeed, more global volatility than in previous ages or eras.

What happens to brands during these periods of turmoil? How do affinity and the principles of branding affect brands during these volatile times?

As we push further into the 21st century, affinity will be more important than ever in building and maintaining brand loyalty. Building a brand is a process, as we have argued. Taking care of a brand is akin to raising a child. It never stops. It is wrought with the unexpected. It demands extra special attention to every detail.

The principles surrounding the brand promise, the fundamental values of the brand, are the philosophy of how a company is run. Maintaining commitments to the brand promise and to the values that influence behaviour are fundamental even before affinity kicks in. Consumers always act in their own self-interest and if a brand ceases to provide better value than existing competition, affinity will dissipate and loyalty will decrease. Companies can never let up their guard on their commitment to value and quality.

The key secret to branding success is to maintain quality advantage and tell that story that gives the consumer a reason to remain loyal. Quality exists at every price point in the marketplace in every product and so does value. You cannot tell a story that is not true or is not the whole truth. The consumer will find out. For example, as we suggested in one of our case studies, this is what happened when Toyota introduced the new Toyota in Europe and created expectations that were not fulfilled, or as we explained in another case study when Ford introduced its new Thunderbird.

Value is always in the consumer perspective and for many it is the trigger for consumer decision-making. Brand equals tangible plus intangible attributes over price. Value also equals tangible plus intangible attributes over price. In this sense, brand equals value. This value equation is fundamental to branding and it is at the root of the ability to tell stories that create affinity.

The recent experience at Toyota is instructive. Recall after recall after recall...but then an increase in car sales of 35 per cent in the month of March 2010! Why so many recalls in quick succession? Automobile companies make decisions on whether a fault is systemic and deserves a general recall or is an occasional problem that affects few owners. In the latter case, the problem is dealt with when it occurs. In most cases, automobile companies deal with problems on a random continuous basis.

Toyota car owners reported that they had acceleration problems. But Toyota was not transparent in its response to the problem. They equivocated in their response. The problem spiralled out of control and led to a congressional hearing, class-action lawsuits, a humiliating appearance by the CEO, Mr. Toyoda, before the Congressional Committee, apologies and more. In the midst of this major brand crisis, Toyota tried to find a way out. They finally decided on a major recall program.

During the same period of turmoil at Toyota, other car companies, such as Ford, Chrysler and Honda, have also had problems and they chose to deal with those problems by recall programs. But it was Toyota that made the news and remained in the public spotlight with so many recalls.

The question is, do recalls hurt brand reputation? There was so much negative publicity surrounding the Toyota recalls and public criticism about Toyota's behaviour prior to its recalls. Surprisingly, at the same time, Toyota sales are reported to have increased substantially. How can one explain this apparent contradiction? Toyota adopted an aggressive and compelling solution to their problem. They cut prices to be very competitive with Ford and other automobiles in the marketplace. Toyota cars have performed well for so long. Most Toyota owners are very satisfied with their cars. Toyota owners recognize the value and performance of their vehicles over time. There remains a great deal of goodwill even with all the headlines and negative publicity surrounding Toyota. If Toyota product continues to demonstrate value through superior quality and competitive pricing, many consumers will still opt for Toyota.

Toyota has publicly recommitted itself to value and quality. That has been their global message. They have publicly put value into the brand equation. Since millions of consumers have been satisfied with their Toyota experience, Toyota's actions have created competitive relevance. The consumer has recognized this. That competitive relevance has resulted in increased sales.

We have argued that one of the primary attributes of affinity is personality. Many people experience misfortune. Yet, most people recover. They persevere and they recover. Their personality overcomes these instances of misfortune leading to recovery.

In Toyota's case, personality contributed to building a rapid recovery. We can speak of the characteristics of the Toyota personality – tenacity, innovation, perseverance, determination and commitment to quality. These characteristics of the Toyota personality, the ingredients of their affinity, were built up over decades, refined by experience and tested globally. These characteristics don't go away quickly. They are still at the root of the Toyota brand personality. They became the basis of effective action on the part of Toyota in facing the recent crisis and defined their actions in PR, pricing and service.

Toyota has now harnessed all the affinity created for the brand in the past and it is now working for Toyota. There is a great deal of goodwill among Toyota owners who want Toyota to succeed. They have a personal commitment to the brand and that commitment will serve Toyota well.

Products have life cycles. In the case of automobiles, that life cycle is approximately six years. Technology changes, innovation drives transformations, aesthetics change and public taste changes. The competition in the auto sector globally is fierce and becoming fiercer as new competitors emerge.

There is no doubt that Toyota today faces serious challenges. Will consumer loyalty be sustained in the face of recent experience? Are Toyota products reaching the end of their viable life cycle? Will the competition outclass and outperform Toyota products? The challenge for Toyota with its existing owner body is that when they come to look at a new Toyota, it must be better in terms of features and quality than existing Toyotas. But it must also be fully competitive with other cars in the category. It is wise to remember that Toyota has had the best customer loyalty rates in the industry. That fact should serve Toyota well into the near future.

In addition, Toyota owners have a stake in their commitment to Toyota. The residual value of their vehicles is a function of how successful Toyota is now and in the future. People act in their own self-interest. Customer loyalty to Toyota helps maintain residual value in their existing cars. Affinity to the brand helps sustain this customer loyalty.

Finally, Toyota does recognize the brand equation we have discussed before. This brand equation needs to be nurtured. Toyota acted to overcome their image issue by decreasing the price of their vehicles and in so doing they strengthened the value of Toyota for the consumer. Simultaneously, they addressed their image question and enhanced their value equation. Their marketing actions so far have proved successful. Toyota will remain strong because of the principles in its brand promise of superior quality and the values and personality that drive day-to-day activities of the company.

During these times of economic volatility and corporate adjustments, Ford appears to be a big winner in the vehicle sector. We should remember that Ford trucks always sustained their quality and always had strong market share in Europe, North America and South America. Ford's commitment to quality trucks never wavered. Cars were different. In cars, as we have pointed out, design trumped quality. In the Q 1 campaign that ran for eleven years, Ford stated, repeatedly, "Quality is Job #1." The brilliance of that advertising is that it publicly committed management to quality. It was the brand promise – expressed publicly. When this advertising campaign ceased, it seemed as if the commitment to quality waned in cars, not in trucks. Ford never stopped telling stories about Ford Tough trucks. But it seems as if Ford had no consistent brand promise for cars. As a result it did not create affinity for their cars in the same way as it did for trucks.

When Ford hired Alan Mulally as the president and CEO, he quickly made quality the core foundation for the future of Ford. Quality became not only an internal rallying cry but it appeared in Ford automobile advertising everywhere. Ford began to tell quality stories about its cars in advertising and public relations. These stories are beginning to have an effect and to create affinity for the Ford brand. At the same time as reasserting its commitment to quality, Ford is trying to win market share with aggressive incentives that create better value.

The examples of Toyota and Ford are valuable insights as to how to deal with brand issues during periods of market turmoil and volatility.

It is, of course, interesting to speculate about the viability of brands during periods of intense volatility. Will Goldman Sachs survive? Will they suffer? The Goldman Sachs brand has produced results for their clients in the past. As long as they can demonstrate that they can produce results for those clients, in the near term they may suffer a little, but in the longer term they will prosper. Goldman may be bruised. But they too have a personality characterized by client commitment, talent, brilliance and the service they provide for customers. During this time of volatility, their customers may blink, but will likely stay with them because they make money for their customers. They deliver on their brand through performance.

In branding and affinity, price continues to remain a great equalizer. Is SONY losing out to Samsung? The question is not that SONY is losing affinity, but rather that Samsung now provides more innovative products at more competitive prices. Mercedes and BMW both introduced C-segment cars that do not have the same features as their top-of-the line vehicles. But these cars carry the Mercedes and BMW brands at lesser than luxury price points. When the mass market is the target even with luxury brands, price becomes a factor.

Brands are like children. They need constant affection, care, nurturing and also investment. This process never ends. It is a continuous commitment. If a company thinks it can cheapen the product, for example, by using cheaper plastic in a car, or a cheaper fabric for seats, it will encourage its owner base to look elsewhere. Today, consumers feel no guilt or anxiety in looking elsewhere in their search for quality and fair pricing. The new age of information-sharing, social networks, blogs and Google encourages this kind of foraging for quality and fair pricing. The sustainability of brand and affinity is very precarious in this era of volatility and market turmoil.

chapter thirty-five

Some Further Extensions

-- -- -- -- -- -- -- -- -- -- -- -- -- --

Branding is now part of everyday vocabulary. Can you take the approach to branding outlined in this book and apply it to universities, political parties, countries and/or religious institutions? Individuals are part of all these and they necessarily are part of the branding process. Companies have brands. Institutions such as universities are now using the language of branding. Political parties have adopted the language of branding. Countries have brands by utilizing the "Made in…" slogan. Can we extend the logic of branding to individuals themselves? How far can we go?

Branding has transformed both the context of individual behaviour and also individual behaviour, itself. Today, individuals are part of many things. We all participate in the brand world, whether we admit it or not. As consumers we engage in totemic activity by buying Apple, Nike, Blackberry and SONY, etc. We cannot escape. These brands define individuals in every consumer society, from New York to Beijing, from Paris to Delhi, from Johannesburg to Santiago. This global brand world affects how we act, what we drink, how we perceive ourselves, and it defines our expectations of ourselves. We all participate in this branding world. Actively or passively, by an act of will or by osmosis, we absorb the values of this brand-driven world of consumerism.

In a previous chapter, we have argued that the globalization of brands and products have converged with the evolution of social networks to create a global consumer who participates in a new global consumer network. In this new world, evaluation of products and brand experience is unmediated, direct and immediate. The viral video of a runaway Toyota Prius in California was everywhere. YouTube is just the beginning. Virtual/viral videos are emerging as the new evaluative marketplace for products, brands and inventions. There we can access directly the good, the bad and the ugly. Everything is open and at play in this new virtual/viral marketplace. The new, robust, global consumer has found his or her playing field and it is global, available to everyone, anywhere. Most importantly, it is immediate, honest, direct and based on personal experience. It is up to anybody and everybody to "take it or leave it" but it is out there!

The maturing consumer wants a lot. At one time, honesty was sufficient. It meant not telling a lie. But a grey area remained. You may not have told a lie, but today, we demand more. We want to see everything; we demand transparency. We are now demanding that corporations and also politicians and people reveal everything, that they volunteer everything, up front. Transparency is revealing everything, holding nothing back and in those circumstances, everybody engages in and can be expected to be cross-examined.

We expect guarantees for our products. We want answers from politicians. We want loyalty from our friends. We want the powerful to be humbled. We want the Catholic Church's secrets revealed. And...more.

In the new age of global consumerism the power to cross-examine is one of the important functions of instant communications including social networks. We are beginning to learn that people, institutions, corporations, even the Catholic Church, are obliged to tell their stories, the entire story, the truth: we want everything revealed!

The consequence of this, we have argued, is that the values of transparency and voluntarism must now become grafted onto the value structure and the governing structure of global corporations. If a global corporation wants its global brands to survive or thrive, they must accept these new values. In 2010, Toyota has learned this painfully and is experiencing this transformation. Others will have to follow.

The new social networks are creating a new consumer society and a different kind of marketplace. Both are global in scope and reach. But the engines that propel them and the engineers who drive them are very, very local. You and I speak with our "friends" on Facebook. We are the community, but we participate in the global marketplace. Indeed, there is a renaissance of empowerment taking place in global consumerism where the consumer can take on Toyota and make Mr. Toyoda apologize publicly!

The new global consumerism is now demanding fairness, transparency and openness. The renovation of corporate values is being moved forward by this new global consumer.

There is a new discipline that is emerging within this context. Corporations are undergoing very intensive self-evaluation. Even GM had to do it. It was painful, of course. But it had to be done. Toyota is now doing it. Self-evaluation must be done in the open for public witnesses. What is the brand promise? What are the values that are tied to and define the brand promise? What are the attributes that emerge from a commitment to certain values?

One of the important consequences of the new e-society demonstrated by social networks is that people are also engaged in a process both of self-expression and public evaluation. And this is done within the court of "friends" and on personal "walls" where your self-expression is followed by the immediate evaluation of you by others! Everything up front and known! You are the product placed into the public space. You volunteer to enter this new open, public space. You are open to comment, evaluation, praise, blame and everything in between. Most importantly, this court of friends creates a new person. People are feeling comfortable within this new environment. You express yourself, you allow yourself to be scrutinized and you comment on others.

This public process of self-expression, evaluation and scrutiny is becoming a habit. And habits change the way we think of ourselves. They also change the values we have. Values affect behaviour; they are the guiding principles of behaviour. If the process we are now engaged in of self-expression and evaluation within the court of "friends" and on personal "walls" is indicative, then we may anticipate some perceptible change in values.

The way of doing politics is also changing very rapidly. It is not just a matter of communication. Political parties, governments and politicians used to be ensnarled in the matrix of communication, getting the message out first, putting the right "spin" on the message, advertising. There is much more to the world of communication now than before. The world of "friends" and "walls," YouTube and Twitter, and much more, now craft the messages and are the vehicles of communication. The war in politics must be waged in these trenches now. The world of influence is much, much more complex and fragmented than before.

In the world of "friends" people feel they have a "say," their opinions are not just known and read, but are shared. Their opinions have consequence. It is an extension of empowerment. You are not just a statistic in some survey, but your views are "posted" on a "wall" for others to see! You are engaged in a discourse and you are "friends" with others. This too is a part of the new consumerism, the new global consumerism.

The consequences for democracy are enormous. The genius of democracy is to trust the people. The genius of democracy is that there is public wisdom. The belief in democracy is that you can find the collective consensus and through a process, whether it is in the marketplace or by elections or in Parliament, the collective consensus can be found and holds sway in the public interest.

People vote for themselves; they act in their own self-interest. But it is the marketplace that filters these self-interests and forges the public interest. That is what is so seductive about the democratic process and voting. It asserts that you can act in your own self-interest yet, at the same time, you can have a hand in forging the public good.

Doing politics is engineering public consent. In actively participating in the "doing" of politics, you contribute to the engineering of consent. That is the magnet for many people and that is what is so endlessly attractive about the democratic political game.

The globalization of consumerism may well be anathema to some. It may also be thought dangerous to others. But, at least for the moment, there appears to be an endless urge from all parts of the world to get into the consumer age, to expand consumerism and the instruments of this expansion are global brands.

However, the emergence of the culture of global consumerism, indeed, itself is an act of democratization. Power is now shifting towards the consumer. Marx may have said you are what you eat. But today, you are also what you consume. The consumer society is on a "tear." The globalization of the consumer marketplace is teaching more and more people a set of values that have enormous consequences.

Global companies produce global products and create global consumers. Global consumers now share common values that they are learning to enforce on global companies. This in turn affects the way global products are now made and has an impact on the internal culture of global companies. Values drive behaviour and we have argued that the global consumer marketplace witnesses the globalization of consumer values.

Emerging patterns and values in the global, interconnected consumer market become habits and are then grafted onto cultures. Is it possible that the same values may be extended from the global consumer world to the political world? Are we witnessing the flow, infiltration and emerging coincidence of values from global consumerism to politics?

Globalization influences consumer expectations of products. You introduce digital cameras and you change the meaning and use of cameras. Innovation and new products drive global consumption. Common consumer values emerge and drive consumer behaviour. Common values drive purchasing behaviour in almost every culture. Globalization of consumer products leads to globalization of needs and globalization of values as it relates to consumer products.

Does this same pattern apply to politics? Can we see the

process of the globalization of political values as we have witnessed the globalization of consumer values? Global consumer values are now emerging and being diffused quickly as a consequence of e-society. Is the same process taking place as people share their ideas and therefore begin to both share and shape common political values? Is political culture following consumer culture? Can we anticipate a globalizing of political culture emerging from the new globalized consumer culture?

The challenge always remains the same. How to ask the right questions and where to look for the clues to appropriate answers? What drives behaviour? Then, how to influence behaviour? There are always clues. Stories...we must find and listen to the stories that people are telling. Embedded in the stories are threads that when woven together do reveal the values. These values drive behaviour. Wells...we must find the "wells" and study the "wells" of contemporary existence. In the matrix of the new "wells" of contemporary society, in the social networks, lie the many stories and values, the many modes of communication. Games...there seems to be a proliferation and a globalization of the games that cultures engage in and that influence behaviour. Even games have become global: The Olympics, World Cup of soccer, Internet poker and many more. Gossip and social networks...we must pay very close attention to the evolution of social networks. Technologies of communication are pushing more and more people into these endless webs where individuality is effectively played out and new forms of individual and collective efficacy are being defined. These new webs have enormous influence on all aspects of behaviour. Young people...the trendsetters of the global consumer culture always are the barometers of the coming times and remain important whenever we want to study social structures.

A global world of friends, no longer tied to a neighbourhood...the well where we shared stories and gossip is global now, not local. You are what you share with friends everywhere. As you now share your experience with consumer products with others, you also share political thought and your experience in social networks. The consumer world intersects with and absorbs the political world...affinity ties it all together.

Acknowledgements

My approach is predicated on an understanding of how people behave, how culture plays a huge role in people's behaviour. It is this cultural approach to study consumer and political behaviour that gave me a point of view in helping our clients bring products, ideas and politicians to the marketplace. I once said, fortunately or unfortunately, "You sell politicians like tomatoes." I was chastised for this observation when it appeared in the press. However, brands often need affinity to succeed and so does a politician. What you say, what attracts and attaches people are fundamental to brand-building and affinity.

Certain scholars had a huge impact on my thinking and left an indelible mark on how I approach problems: Margaret Mead, Ruth Benedict, Bronislaw Malinowski, Georg Zimmel, Robert K. Merton, Talcott Parsons, C.W. Mills and Everett Hughes. These thinkers gave us a theoretical framework to understand culture and to interpret what people say. What people say is interpreted within a framework of a theoretical understanding of behaviour.

I was fortunate to have many mentors, people who trusted and believed in me and were prepared to identify with my approach and helped me to develop it. In politics, Senator Keith Davey was key. He hired me to become the Liberal Party pollster in 1972. He believed in what I did

298

and never wavered through the good times and the difficult times. I learned about loyalty, commitment, discipline and ideals from Senator Davey. His friendship was sincere and uncompromising. We worked together for many years and through many elections. I have a great deal to thank him for. He was not only a unique, amazing political advocate, but for me he was a true mentor.

It was through Senator Davey that I became known as Trudeau's pollster. That was a very unique and special relationship that lasted for 12 years. My special relationship with Prime Minister Trudeau gave me an international profile that allowed me to function in the international business world.

There were other political mentors, as well. Among them were Tom Axworthy, Jim Coutts and Michael Kirby. In the advertising world, there was Terry O'Malley, Bill Bremner and so many others. The great thing about being involved in politics is the people you meet, the ideas you share and exchange and the long-term memories and friendships that endure.

I was also very fortunate to have mentors in the business world: in Canada, John New, Peter Godsoe and Larry Nadler; in the United States, John Morrissey, Ray Ablondi, Bob Rewey, Ross Roberts, Bud Coughlan, Bobbie Gaunt and Mark Hutchins; in Europe, Ian McAllister, Duncan Rouke, Massimo Ghenzer, Andrea Formica and Udo Khal.

My daughter, Alonna, has worked closely with me for

many years in market research at Goldfarb Consultants and Goldfarb Intelligence Marketing and also at The Goldfarb Corporation. She has made an enormous contribution to the way I think. My daughter Rebecca has also made significant contributions to this manuscript.

One person, my wife, Joan, has been more than a mentor. She has supported me in every endeavour and has always encouraged me to pursue my dreams.

Mentoring, I believe, was a huge part of my success. These people and others trusted and admired my work. We enjoyed spending time together. We shared ideas. We explored and challenged each other's thinking – all to the benefit of producing better strategies and communications for the client.

Ideas for the most part are not enough. Unique, tangential thinking is required and the challenge is to create ideas that can actually be implemented. Implementation is the genius of marketing, not the idea alone. My success was predicated on having talented clients who were willing to implement some of the ideas and strategies that we developed. Their implementation made me successful.

In my experiences in politics, I learned some simple fundamentals. Elections are fought on dreams and fears. Fear and guilt are important motivations in behaviour. And dreams, such as the Canadian commitment to the North, Canadian self-sufficiency, Canadian independence and Canadian nationalism are true motivators.

Martin Goldfarb